JOHN LEAX

Grace Is Where I Live

THE LANDSCAPE OF FAITH & WRITING

WORDFARM

LA PORTE, INDIANA

WordFarm
2010 Michigan Avenue
La Porte, IN 46350
www.wordfarm.net
info@wordfarm.net

–Scripture quotations are from The Holy Bible, King James Version.

Cover Image: iStockPhoto

Design: Andrew Craft

USA ISBN 0-9743427-2-6

Printed in the United States of America

First WordFarm Edition: 2004

Libray of Congress Cataloging-in-Publication Data

Leax, John.
  Grace is where I live: the landscape of faith & writing / John Leax.—Expanded ed.
    p. cm.
  ISBN 0-9743427-2-6
  1. Leax, John. 2. Authors, American—20th century—Biography. 3. Christian biography—United States. 4. Creative writing. I. Title.

BR1725.L264A3 2003
277.3'082'092—dc22
[B]

                                                                      2003064626

P   17   16   15   14   13   12   11   10   9   8   7   6   5   4   3   2   1
Y   17   16   15   14   13   12   11   10   09   08   07   06   05   04

"Leax writes an unvarnished prose, easy and graceful and blunt all at once."

—Walter Wangerin Jr.

"*Grace Is Where I Live* abounds in plainspoken profundity."

—Paul J. Willis

"*Grace Is Where I Live* is an engaging and informative series of reflections upon aspects of the writer's identity and art. In the informal and intimate tradition of the personal essayist, John Leax invites the reader to share his life and the experiences that shaped his vocation as a writer. In the course of doing so he leads us through the critical questions that [all writers] serious about . . . vocation must ask—and especially those committed to a Christian worldview.

"Leax's reasoned scrutiny of the steps that led him to become a writer could well spare some students the particular anguishes and cul-de-sacs that lie in wait for those tugged in several vocational directions. The chapter 'Giving Up Everything' I think is especially valuable in this regard—it goes to the heart of the matter."

—Robert Siegel

"While Leax belongs by commitment and heritage to the evangelical community (both his 'primary audience' and his 'most troubling' one), he echoes the work of no other writer in the stables of evangelical publishing. 'I am less and less sure of what I have to say,' he muses. One thing he knows is that 'language and reality are inextricably bound.' With that as a given, he sees three possible 'strategies.' He can 'choose silence . . . the way of the mystic and my late dog, Poon.' He can accept 'the language of [his] culture group as final, and . . . speak cliches and platitudes.' Or he can 'consciously choose the creative responsibility of language.' The latter is clearly his choice."

—Shirley Nelson in *The Christian Century*

"John Leax makes the most promising attempt I have seen to enlighten novice writers, and he does it in a refreshingly lucid prose, unpolluted with the ego that so often finds its way into the best writers' words."

—Virginia Stem Owens in *Christianity Today*

liberal (B Graham)

Grace Is Where I Live

"Giving Up Everything" appeared in *Reality and the Vision* edited by Philip Yancey (Dallas, Texas: Word, 1990). Used with permission.

"Dream" appeared in *Country Labors* by John Leax (Grand Rapids, Michigan: Zondervan, 1991). Used with permission.

"Story, Place and Marriage" first appeared in the Spring 1991 issue of *Marriage Partnership*.

"Vow" appeared in the Spring 2003 issue of *Christianity and Literature*.

Other essays in this book appeared in *Arkenstone, The Wellsville Daily Reporter, Christian Life* and *The Reformed Journal*.

For Lionel Basney
1946-1999

Contents

Preface

When I gathered the essays for the first edition of *Grace Is Where I Live*, I selected from work that had been written over a period of twenty years. My intention was to shape a summary of what I had learned about writing and vocation and go on to other things. That, in fact, is what I did.

My life in the local community and a new direction in my teaching turned me to writing nature essays and a regular column for a regional newspaper. Much of that work was collected in *Out Walking*. The demands of writing so much prose on short deadlines, however, overwhelmed my imagination and I stopped writing poetry. That made me an unhappy writer and a disconcerted man. After a careful consideration of my gifts, my desires and my vocation, I committed myself to writing only poetry.

When the editors of WordFarm proposed this new edition of *Grace*, I was enthused but sadly lacking in new material to enrich and enliven an old book. Through the spring and into the summer of 2003 I struggled with how to make *Grace* new and avoid writing prose. My struggle was not intense. Mostly I procrastinated, worked in my garden, and completed a long poem. But finally a copy of the text presented to me by Jane Miner, the secretary of the Houghton College Department of English, who makes my life one of ease, forced me to read my own words and do something constructive.

In the last essay of *Grace*, "In the Care of the Spirit," I found a way to proceed. In it I identified three themes that have shaped my life as a writer: incarnation, the place of the human in the physical world, and the meaning of community. In the ten years since completing the first edition of *Grace* I have ceased to think of them as separate themes and have come to understand them as a single exploration of the presence of God in creation. While I am convinced that this exploration is so fundamental to my life as a Christian that it would have focused my attention had I never written a word, I am also convinced that for me writing has been the best way to discovery and faith.

For this edition of *Grace* I have added a small number of essays that carry forward this single theme while simultaneously reflecting on the act of writing as a means to discovering grace.

I began the first edition of *Grace* with a poem, "What I Have Found," that looked back and set the tone of summary I intended. I want to close this edition with another poem, "Vow," to indicate an active looking ahead to more and better work.

John Leax
Fillmore, New York
November 5, 2003

Introduction

$\mathcal{W}$hen I was a student at Wheaton College, Chad Walsh visited campus to read his poems and to lecture. I was impressed. He was the first poet I'd ever heard read, and his performance was masterful. Not only did his poems hang before me in the air like mist in sunlight, but his commentary on them opened the life behind the poems to me. During the question and answer period after his reading, he was asked how one became a Christian writer. I'm surprised I can't remember the exact words of his answer, for I have come to live by its logic: if one is a Christian, one will be a Christian writer; it is impossible for it to be otherwise.

Those brief remarks constituted the full extent of the instruction I was offered as I tried to find my way to maturity both as a Christian and as a writer. Wise as they were, and adequate to me as they are now, they were not enough when I was twenty. I wanted and needed to hear more. I needed to hear what it might mean to submit my life and my words to the Lordship of Jesus Christ. I needed to hear extensive testimony from those who had gone before me about the struggles, trials and rewards of the vocation of writing. I needed good news.

In writing this book I have remembered my difficulty as a student, and with my students in mind I have consciously written the book I didn't have thirty years ago when I needed it. Had I been given it then, I probably wouldn't have liked it; I would have found it too conservative. But I would have read it and fought with it, and that is what I hope my students and other readers will do with it: read it and fight with it. I have written personally; I am not a theorist—my experience is not definitive. In these pages I offer one writer's testimony to be placed beside the testimony of other writers, men and women, and tested by comparison.

I believe in what I have written, but I know I have written only part of the truth. Much remains to be discovered in practice.

Parts one and two of the book treat questions of vocation. The first three essays consider particular relationships. What does it mean to live a holy life? How does one's craft contribute to that holiness? What is the meaning of witness? How does one use language to a purpose without compromising its integrity? What is the meaning of place and community? How does one speak for and to that community? These three essays are reflective and tend to be summative with strong conclusions suggesting I know what I'm talking about. They are essays to be argued with. "Giving Up Everything," the last essay of part one, is a retrospective discussion of what, at a particular point in time, I understood I was personally called to do and to be.

Part two is an edited version of a journal I kept for two or three months immediately following the completion of "Giving Up Everything." The struggle recorded in these pages belongs in this collection because it is partner to the surety expressed in the reflective essays. Only by placing the two side by side can I begin to say the dynamic of my experience.

Part three explores what working in three literary genres has meant to me. Implicit in the discussion is my sense that each genre inclines a writer to a perspective unique to it and a sense that all genres are necessary to a full expression of human experience.

Part four was originally going to be titled "Continuities." In it I intended to tie together the themes of part three and make a comprehensive statement about what I have been trying to do in my writing. I have a clear sense that over time and over genres my concerns have been guided and focused by the Spirit I have sought to follow. To testify to that is important to me. But as I approached actually saying what I think they are and making some kind of summative statement, I felt a great reluctance. Such a statement is not mine to make; it is a critic's. For me to sum up in absolute fashion a process that is continuing would be both presumptuous and deadening. But I did want to think about the direction such a statement might take. Consequently, I turned, as I have in the past, to the journal format to explore an open topic. Here, however, I have done something slightly different from before. Rather than setting out over a period of time to write on a theme, I have gone back into my notebooks and taken stories and excerpts that connect small but formative experiences with my growing understanding of my themes and concerns.

The story may be apocryphal, but I've heard that Mickey Spillane once said to Edward R. Murrow, "I write the kind of books I want to read that no one else writes." Whatever one may think of Mickey Spillane, he has a point. In one way or another, all writers write what they want to read.

If in writing these essays I have been writing for my students, I have also been writing for myself. Like Mickey Spillane, I have been writing the book I want to read now. I still need to hear, no longer what it might mean to submit my life and my words to the Lordship of Jesus Christ, but what it means to have tried and to be trying. I have written to explore and test what I think I know and to discover what I don't know.

Writing this way, I have made a marker for myself that reads, "This is where I am." I have made a marker that reads, "This is the place from which I proceed."

What I Have Found

This place that claims my midlife
labor is not an Eden I have made.
It is a place of trial.
My hope resides in yielding
to what calls me still to stay.

No charming serpent curls
about my arm and whispers
in my ear. But I am tempted
nonetheless. Like Homer
I take the stories of my people,
I give them shape, and hand
them down. What I pass on
is truth made new—half-truth
spun through kind invention.

The world I make is finer
than the world I know. How else
contain the bitterness, the pain,
the grief? I have not lied.

I say my words; I seek
the wholeness of the world.
Like Homer I am blind.
I see what is not here.
I see this place by word
and grace a new creation.
That word is what I've found.
That grace is where I live.

Part One

Holiness and Craft

*The approach of a man's life out
of the past is history, and the
approach of time out of the future
is mystery. Their meeting is the
present, and it is consciousness,
the only time life is alive.*

Wendell Berry
The Long-Legged House

The Presbyterian church I attended in the mid-1950s was a small, dark brown brick chapel surrounded by trees and a graveyard with markers dating to the Revolution. It was a quiet church, bearing little resemblance to the sprawling suburban structure it has become. Musicals and pageants, three- and four-choir spectaculars, and dramatic readings have replaced strawberry festivals, occasional solos and sermons on "The Way of the Cross."

I reached the age of accountability, learned the Westminster Catechism and the Apostles' Creed, made a public confession of faith, celebrated my first Communion, and joined the church just before the change. Consequently, I didn't benefit from the expanded program and sudden relevance. I was required to study the content of Scripture and the foundations of Christian orthodoxy.

The emphasis on learning was interesting, for it did not require me to conform to any specified pattern of behavior. I discovered Christianity is a matter of willing God's will and through Christ becoming one with it. I like to think that a conscious application of Augustine's principle "Love God and do as you please" was behind the emphasis, but I suspect the truth is the church failed to grasp the ethical implications of the gospel. At any rate, as a youth I did pretty much as I pleased, and I can recall little to be ashamed of in my behavior. So, deliberate or accidental, the emphasis was sound.

It was sound, I think, because in my father I had an example of wholeness, of what a person by conscious effort might become. I didn't know it then, and I am only coming to understand it now, but his life was a pursuit of holiness worked out in terms of devotion, faithfulness and craft.

The fall after my tenth birthday I began to take trumpet lessons. My teacher was an impatient man who would stomp around the back room of the music store where he taught, clasping his ears and muttering, "Oh my God, my God," as I played. At home the reaction to my glorious noise was less dramatic and usually took the form, "Get back in there and practice." As Christmas approached, however, my father began to spend more and more time in the basement. I wondered if he was feeling the same anguish as my music teacher, but each time I visited him I found him quietly working, fitting together small pieces of white pine. He refused to say what he was making, but he impressed me with the way he worked. Though his hands were quick and sure—the clean wood curled in amazing spirals from his plane—he did not rush. Time seemed unimportant—even suspended. What mattered was the smoothness of the wood and the tightness of the fit. Christmas morning I learned what I had watched him make. Beside the tree, holding my music book, was a wooden music stand more carefully shaped than any note I would ever play.

That music stand, as meaningful as it has become, was a small thing compared to the work to which my father gave his life. Shortly after making it, he and my mother picked out and bought four treeless acres twenty miles outside of Pittsburgh. Then, working long evenings and weekends, they began the slow discipline of building and making a place worthy of the word *home*. I was old enough to help and learned in aching arms and legs the weight of the gravel that lies underneath the concrete slab the house rests on. I learned the weight of the studs, the Celotex and the plywood. I learned how many nails go into the side of a house. And with each wheelbarrow load of gravel, with each stack of studs, with each sheet of Celotex or plywood, with each driven nail, I learned the cost and labor of a shelter from the weather. It was a good lesson, one I consider and cherish as I work maintaining my own place. But that was only part of the lesson I learned.

The house, as it was built, was alien—a glaring construction stuck by aliens on the surface of a field. The house had to become more than a house; it had to become a place at once on and in the field. The long process of growing into and being accepted by the land began. I speak of that process in a poem.

Like an army preparing a siege
the woods mass
around my father's acres.

They've taken the cornfields,
the neighbor's orchard and swept
across the field of winter wheat
that bowed like a congregation
kneeling in the wind.

No farmer seeking profit
from the land, my father
had no quarrel with woods.
His code read, Love your enemies.
He cast his lot against the grain;
he planted trees.
The dogwood, maple, hemlock
and tulips rooted
with my youth have prospered
in his soil and rise
twenty feet above his roof.

Outflanked, the woods have lost.
Ordered and in place,
they shade his evening's rest.

Two years ago my father died. Last Thanksgiving I drove from my home in the wide, comfortable valley of the Genesee River down through the mountains and narrow valleys of Pennsylvania to those acres. It was probably the last time I will ever drive those particular roads, for I was going to help my mother move from that place of their making to a new place which would be one of her making. I approved completely of her move. Yet it was hard to think of that house and those acres without one of us.

Early Friday morning I walked outside and stood on the back porch. A pair of black-capped chickadees scratched in the circle of sunflower seeds spilled under the feeder. No other birds would tolerate my closeness, but I knew, even in their absence, the presence of the squabbling bluejays and voracious grosbeaks that had spilled the seeds. I knew the presence of the hummingbirds that sought out the Joseph's Coat and the maligned starlings and grackles that sparkled purple and blue in the sun. Down the bank from the feeder I could see the fish pond my father and I had dug one Sunday afternoon. Its water was dark and acid from the maple leaves fallen into it from a sapling we had planted that now rises thirty or forty feet in height. I went down the bank, past the pond and across the lawn toward the forsythia hedge and the gate to the pasture. The lawn where we had played ball was thick with trees—small maples, evergreens, walnuts and others I do not know. Just before I reached the hedge, I stopped. At my feet was the feeder where my father had kept cracked corn for the pheasants. I remembered looking out the windows on winter mornings and seeing ringnecks and hens clustered like barnyard fowl around the corn. I remembered the pleasure my father took in drawing them to the yard. Raising my eyes, I looked through the hedge and over the gate to where he had kept a salt block to attract deer. It was gone.

I went through the gate—the ghosts of Brutus, the big grey gelding, and Chico, the small, brilliant Arabian palomino, cantering up to me for carrots and conversation. Suddenly two deer exploded—white tails flashing—from the brush beyond the barn and bolted up the back hill. They paused once near the top, turned to look back, then disappeared over the crest into the woods. I turned and walked back to the house. The lesson my father had been teaching me by his life was complete.

The place he had made, as I viewed it that morning, was not the end of his life. His end was to achieve something far more difficult to measure and price than an "estate." His end was to realize the moment of building and to live a full and abundant life in the only time life is alive, the present. As a result, he was free of the burden of the future, free of the burden of finishing that diminishes the working. And free of those burdens, he was free to concentrate on the act of working. He was free to reach for holiness. I say reach for holiness because ultimately holiness is never achieved. It is setting one's mind in the direction of God. It is setting aside what one is to become what God wills. This setting aside does not imply discontinuity. The new—that is, the present—is based on the past. One can only become what one already is. "In my beginning is my end," said T. S. Eliot.

All of this so far has been an effort to define my life in relation to my father's life and in relation to my past. It is an essay in personal history. What I've set down, I've discovered as I've written. What remains to be written, I must discover as I write. The attempt to re-create the past and make it live in the present is an attempt to live consciously, to know where my life is going by understanding where it has been, to know what I might become by knowing what I am.

I've written as if my father and I were alike. In many ways we are. But in an important way we are not. I remember the day he told me he had never read a work of fiction, not even Hemingway's *The Old Man and the Sea*, which I had given to him. I felt a personal loss. I live by saying my world in poems. My father lived his life without words. He rarely rose to self-consciousness. What his hands could touch was all the world he needed.

Yet even in this difference there is a likeness, for my father was a craftsman who cared more for the act of making, for the assault on perfection, than for the finished product. And it was in his work, not in the products of his work, that he approached holiness. I am learning the same is true for me, though I work not in wood but in words.

Here I must make some distinctions. Three paragraphs ago I said I discover what I have to say as I write. This is crucial to my thinking. It is also crucial to my becoming. But it is not what I am speaking of now. The discovery of what I have to say, of what my poem or essay means, is, like the poem or essay itself, the product of my work. It is not my work.

As I write, the poem I am writing is always in the future. When I have finished writing, it is behind me. It is in the past. Only as I am writing it, as it is in the process of becoming, is it in the present. And only as it is in the present, is it my concern. Compare this to salvation. Salvation is a process occurring in all three tenses. It is future because it will not be complete until Christ returns. It is past because Christ accomplished it on the cross. It is present as I give myself to Christ. Here, as in the writing of a poem, my concern is with my present action. What is past is related to the present only as the present brings its meaning into being. What is future is related to the present only as it is imagined and desired in the present—that is, as it is part of the present.

Holiness and craft come together at this point: the moment of the poem is also the moment of salvation. Both occur in the present. I make my way as a poet and as a Christian by giving my attention to being in Christ and in doing in him the work before me. Quoting Thomas Merton, "It is in the ordinary duties and labors of life that the Christian can and should develop his spiritual union with God."

While hoeing his garden, Saint Francis was approached by a villager who had his own idea about how a saint should spend his time. The villager demanded of Francis, "What would you be doing if you knew the Lord would return this afternoon?" Francis replied, "I would be hoeing my garden." This I think is the meaning of "Take therefore no thought for the morrow: for the morrow shall take thought for the things of itself" (Matthew 6:34). Care is implied, not carelessness. If the present is lived in Christ, the Creator of this world, we will do nothing to limit the possibilities of the future.

This is not simplistic; this is the meaning of the verb *to be*. This is the work of God.

At twenty, filled with religious jargon and the assurance of salvation, I knew all the answers. I could quote Scripture in response to any question. I believed in Christ, born of the Virgin, crucified, buried, resurrected and coming again. I still do. But as the years pass, I realize these things I affirm are far more mysterious and complex than I ever imagined them being. The hope of the second coming and a future in heaven is just that, a hope, something unseen. What I have is the present here on earth. This present is the life I've been given to live. It is my concern—and my only concern. My work is to be a husband and father, to make a few poems as well as I can make them, and, most of all, by husbanding, fathering and craft, to make a life where Christ can meet himself.

I like this life. I make my way through it learning its meaning as I go.

Stewardship and Witness

One day some years ago I was working on a poem and muttering to myself, as I always do when I'm writing. The poem must have had an explicitly Christian theme, for my daughter, who was seven or eight, overheard me, came into my study and asked, "Daddy, why do you always put Christ in your poems?" I thought for a moment, trying to determine how much of an answer she wanted, and then replied, "Maybe someone who doesn't know Jesus will read one of my poems and come to know him." It seemed to be the right thing to say to a child, but she looked up at me, slowly shook her head and said, "Nope. It won't work. Nobody ever reads your poems."

Some months later I was invited to speak on the topic of Christians and creativity. I chose to emphasize the process rather than the product of creation and argued that Christians creating act out in their lives the image of God the Creator. But I qualified the openness of that argument with an ever-present concern for the content or message of the poem. Though I never said it outright, I saw the purpose of writing poems to be witnessing to a given truth.

In the past couple of years, however, I have come to question the sufficiency of that perspective. As a poet I am involved in a complex of relationships. I am at once united with the world and the Creator of the world and alienated from the world and the Creator of the world. I live halfway, neither lost nor perfected. I am not, at any time in this life, in full possession of Truth. All I have to witness to is the truth of my experience, the erratic process of my becoming a new creation. Another way of putting this is to say that I am involved in discovering my place in an ecology that involves the physical and the spiritual worlds. (It is important to note how intensely personal this process is. I can discover and speak only my own relationships, not the relationships of all humanity.) The only tool I have been given to make my discoveries and then articulate them is language. Without language I can know nothing; it is the foundation of my knowing and of my being known.

I come to my point. Language and message are inextricably bound. The elevation of either above the other in the act of writing inevitably results in the destruction of both. Ultimately, of course, message is more important. C. S. Lewis's statement that "the salvation of a single soul is more important than . . . all the epics and tragedies in the world" is indisputable. But the message of salvation must be communicated in language. The relationship of the two can best be explained by analogy.

Behind my house, where my daughter once had a swing set and my wife a flower bed, I now have a small but carefully planned vegetable garden. Each year, besides tomatoes and salad greens, I grow enough beans, peas, carrots, broccoli and squash to last the winter. I like vegetables, and I'm anxious to grow as many as I can. But I have learned that if I want large crops, I must recognize my dependence on the earth and become the steward of my land. Consequently, the energy I spend in planting and harvesting is slight in comparison to the energy I spend in composting, manuring and mulching. Taking care of the soil, I take care of my crop, and year after year the garden rewards my stewardship with bounty.

The analogy I am drawing is this: Language is the soil in which message grows. Poets must care about message, but they must first be stewards of language. The message is like a seed. It must fall into the ground and die before it can be born into a poem.

Just as the sacrifice of the soil for the crop of one year is ultimately destructive, so the sacrifice of the language to the demands of message is destructive. Like so many other things in life, we must give up even our truth to keep it. Any other course will use up the soil in which we nurture it and guarantee that the future will be impoverished.

Just as I serve the soil so that my garden will remain fertile and grow good crops, when I write I serve the language so it can bear the message I've learned. Curiously, as I seek to make stewardship my concern, my vision clears, and I speak more precisely the presence of Christ in my world.

Story, Place and Marriage

"Put most simply," Linda said, "my place is beside you." I must have registered surprise or confusion, for she continued quickly, "I know it must sound awfully traditional, but I'm your wife." It did sound traditional, and my first response was perversely defensive. I wanted to say, "I've never asked you to play the part of Ruth," but I didn't. I knew instinctively she would have replied, "No one can ask that. It can only be offered." So I listened as she talked, and I began to understand. My question had come from thoughts of landscape, geography and responsibility—my sense of my place on earth. Her answer had come from marriage—her sense of metaphorical, emotional landscape, a place where we dwell in trust and surety. It turned our conversation to faithfulness, intimacy and community.

Thomas Merton wrote, "The basis of human and Christian community *paul isn't married* is marriage." A celibate himself, he obviously did not mean that only the married can enjoy community. He meant, rather, that marriage with its complementary disciplines of exclusiveness and inclusiveness is one of humanity's defining relationships. Our experience of marriage, whether from within or without, is a determining factor in the way we understand our interactions with each other, with the earth and with God. In short, our experience is not only concrete and real, it is analogical. It points to mysteries beyond itself.

For me the way to those mysteries is through story, through considering and articulating the unique series of events in time and place that make up my life. Surprisingly, though I am a writer and storyteller, I did not discover this until a lonely trip away from home to be a visiting professor at an urban school several winters ago.

My room was pleasant enough—the way good motel rooms are pleasant. I actually liked it. But after only a short while it began to close in on me. When I could stand it no longer I went out into the dark to walk. It had been raining, and as I stood beside a six-lane thoroughfare I intended to cross, the pavement glistened in the headlight glare of the cars swishing past me. I imagined each one powered by bottled anger and driven by a fury dedicated to keeping me on the curb. Trapped there, I thought of the minutes-long gaps between cars on Route 19, the main north-south artery through New York's sparsely populated Allegany County where I live. I wanted to be there. I wanted to be home. The urge to retreat to the parking lot, find my car, start it and abandon the week of teaching strange students in a strange city pounded in me like my heart gone wild.

I did not go to my car. I did not even cross the street. There was nothing on the other side I wanted to see. I went back to my room and brooded. For two days I went about outwardly engaging, doing my duties, but inwardly I went unsettled and agitated. On the third day I suddenly understood. What troubled me was a sense of being unknown. In that place I was out of place. A day's drive from home, among people with whom I shared no history, to whom I owed no obligations, I was lost. I tried to recover a sense of myself by remembering home, by placing myself in memory back in the constellation of familiar relationships, but it did not work. Time and distance had cut me loose. So far from Linda, so far from the place where our relationship has been lived, I had only the confining abstractions of my vows to hold me. That frightened me, for isolated as I was, I could have, without check, indulged any impulse, any whim that came upon me.

Reflecting on that time, I have come to think that my lostness was directly related to my daily dependence on the lived narrative of my marriage to give structure to my life. I live not only in the geographic place to which I give primacy but also in that metaphoric, emotional place called a marriage to which Linda gives primacy. I live not only in a place but also in a story.

Linda and I have been married for twenty-five years. We have lived for eighteen of those years in a house just four miles from the two-room apartment we moved into the day after our wedding, and I have taught for twenty-three years at the college where I studied that first year of our life together. We have been and are geographically stable. But, more than that, we have become placed people. We have made deliberate choices to live in relationship to each other, to become a productive household reaching out to our friends and to our place. We have made our choices slowly—one at a time. And we have learned equally slowly the complexity of those choices because we have stayed to see their consequences.

For example, when a large maple tree in our front yard showed signs of stress, I chose to have it taken down. I cut it into stove lengths, split it and burned it in the wood stove. It heated the house for a whole winter. But I have since endured unbearably hot summer nights because the black roof is no longer shaded from the sun, and in autumn I have fewer leaves to mulch the garden.

That decision was small. It affected only my family, a few small comforts and a bit of compost. Other decisions have been of more consequence. They have affected my neighbors, my colleagues at work, the life of the church and the health of the earth. One in particular affected all of these and changed forever my relationship to my community. When New York State chose a farm three miles from my home for a potential nuclear waste dump, I joined with the members of my church in a time of fasting and prayer. We sought direction for our responses. I chose to join my neighbors and a group of activists from around the county in acts of civil disobedience to halt the siting process until remedies could be found in the political realm. Though I was by no means a central figure, I spoke to groups, interceded between disagreeing factions, and wrote poems and essays for local publications. Most important, I discovered among the citizens of my county friends I would never have otherwise met. One morning at a breakfast rally on the site, I looked around the gathered group. I saw farmers, teachers, housewives, students, engineers, poets, musicians, old hippies and pastors standing in snow and sunlight. I saw in them an image of the church, a church without cultural or class distinctions, and I rejoiced. These events, small and large, are parts of my story. They are also, from another perspective, parts of Linda's story. Taken together our stories make up the story of our marriage, a narrative set in a particular place in time.

We bought our house because we could afford it, and I stayed at my teaching because I liked it. Though those reasons remain true, other reasons now govern our choices. We stay in our house because every room of it is rich with memories, every square foot of the yard is marked by commitment and labor. We read our history in a walk from the kitchen to the bedroom, in a stroll from the woodpile to the garden. I stay at my teaching because whatever my college is I have helped make it. I can no longer step aside without stepping aside from myself. My story and my place are connected.

Writing these words, I am aware of how a story such as mine is, if not an aberration, at least unusual in the last years of the twentieth century. Sometimes I wonder if my faithfulness to marriage and place has any relevance at all.

Last winter I attended a luncheon for faculty on my home campus. The speaker was a prominent evangelical who had spoken in chapel on the necessity to become "world Christians." His address had disturbed me, but I wasn't sure why. I planned to listen and be quiet. One of my colleagues, however, challenged him. He began by summarizing, "In your chapel address you stressed the importance of family. Then you advised a kind of homelessness that rejects the pull of family and home in order to become a citizen of the world." The speaker nodded agreement. My colleague continued, "Aren't you contradicting yourself? I think of the work of my friend Jack Leax, who has written about the importance of the place. Isn't rootedness necessary to citizenship?"

The speaker answered that he saw no contradiction: "The airplane and modern communications have made place anachronistic. The family can stay intact apart from home." Though I disagreed with his answer, I understood his point and did not wish to argue. Then he added, "We can't waste time indulging in sentimental attachments to place." Everyone in the room turned to me. No one spoke, but in every staring face I read a challenge.

My defense that day was simple. It remains simple today. A sentimental attachment to place is, like a sentimental love, stupid and useless—a hindrance to genuine relationship. But a sense of place is not sentimental; it is practical and necessary. The mistake is to consider place provincially. While a sense of place is based on local knowledge, it is not limited to local knowledge. It includes a range of places. Within the last few years I have caught bluefish off the coast of Maine, explored the wilderness of Oregon on horseback and hiked a canyon in Texas. The whole earth is my home. But my trips to Maine, Oregon and Texas were short excursions. My ability to claim the whole earth, to claim the global relationship the speaker advocated, is rooted in my connection to a specific place—a house and five acres of woodlot in western New York, where my relationship is concrete and visible. Apart from my local bond, my relationship to the earth is abstract. It is dangerous for it simplifies, and in simplifying it allows the illusion that we live free of the consequences of our choices. This abstraction has brought us to the brink of environmental disaster. It may take us over the brink.

Consider this analogy in relation to marriage and community: I live most intimately with Linda. What I have learned of love in our years together is local. I touch no one the way I touch her. But touching her as I do—my loving her—allows me to love others appropriately. The strict exclusiveness of our relationship is ultimately inclusive. It opens both of us to responsible relationships with others—men and women. It is the concrete foundation of community for us and for those included by our relationship. The same is true of our relationship to the earth.

The value of placedness is clear. Unfortunately the circumstances of modern life make such placedness as I enjoy less and less a possibility for the population at large. What is one caught in the forced mobility of our urban culture to do? The answer, I believe, lies in story. Story and place are connected. Wallace Stegner has made plain in his essays that a place is not a place until it is lived in—until people give it a story. All of us, whether we dwell in a rural backwater, a suburban sprawl or an urban neighborhood, must choose to be people of story and place. For some, story will take precedence, and the connection to place will be changing and tenuous. But tenuous is not abstract. Tenuous means recognizing that one's local knowledge is (as it always is) insufficient and acting accordingly with restraint and care.

There is hope. Today Linda and I are celebrating our twenty-fifth wedding anniversary. But we are not together. I am writing this in that room I fled several winters ago. I am again in that strange city teaching strange students. But neither are as strange as they were, for I am becoming known. And I have learned that though I may be out of my place beyond the limits of my local knowledge, I am not out of my story. These separations have become part of the larger story Linda and I live together. Our history holds me even here.

Giving Up Everything

The language of faith is dangerous. Most of us desire certainty, but like it or not, almost every statement about faith contains a contradiction. Yesterday, for example, Palm Sunday, I sat in church and listened to a sermon on self-denial. And as I listened, I grew gently angry. I thought, "I have lived my life trying to discover the self Christ is making of me. I will not deny what I have learned." I wanted to stop the sermon. I didn't, of course. I sat silent, knowing that the sermon language was shorthand, that the audience knew what was meant and that I, as usual, was being difficult. Perhaps the issue of self-denial was bringing back painful memories. "God writes straight with crooked lines," says a Spanish proverb, and it is true. The line he has traced across my life is all zigs and zags.

At the age of twelve I was a runt of a boy with a soprano voice and a desire to please adults. This desire found its fullest expression in the life of Beulah Presbyterian Church. I remember one Saturday afternoon in particular. I was at the church office helping to fold bulletins for the next morning. The church secretary, making casual conversation, asked me what I wanted to be when I grew up. I answered, without ever having thought of it before that moment, "A minister." When she gushed in response, I knew I'd found my calling. Nothing else that I could imagine could possibly bring that depth of approval. And so I became, in my mind as well as in the minds of adults, the good boy set apart to become a minister. It nearly ruined my life.

But let me jump to a later point of crisis. I did not become a minister; I became a writer and a teacher. For ten years I was an unsettled, apprehensive writer and teacher, unsure of my vocation. Had I missed my true calling? Desiring to settle the matter, I took a sabbatical. During that time I would do two things: I (the potential preacher) would attend classes at Asbury Seminary, and I (the writer) would research a book on the Trappist monk and poet Thomas Merton. Both projects were directed at resolving my unease, for I knew that Merton had spent much of his adult life struggling with the conflicting demands of both a contemplative and an artistic calling.

As part of my research, I scheduled a retreat at the Abbey of Gethsemani where Merton lived out his vocation. And it was during that retreat that I encountered and accepted the self who Christ by his presence had been making and continues to make in me. I kept a journal, recording the events of the crucial day. From Matins, the predawn watch for the coming of Christ, to Compline, the evening yielding of the body to sleep and the care of Christ, I followed the canonical hours that had for twenty-seven years ordered Merton's life.

October 12, 1977. I usually wear a small pewter cross. I couldn't find it when I was dressing this morning, so I called out, "Linda, I can't find my cross." She replied, only half ironically, "I'm sure you'll find it." I did, and I'm wearing it, but here in my tiny room in the Gethsemani guesthouse I wonder about that other cross, the one I'm supposed to take up to follow Christ.

Nothing prepared me for this silence. I expected an absence of sound. I am overwhelmed by a positive presence.

The instruction sheet I was given tells me, "Retreats are made privately." The solitude I feel is a new thing, entirely unlike the solitude of the mountains or the river. It is a terrible confrontation with the noisiness of my own soul and mind. I want to make a noise, go introduce myself to the man down the hall. If I could talk about God, I wouldn't have to face Him. But here in this silence, all the talking is done by God.

Sext, 12:15 pm. The long, narrow white church is filled with light. During the service, bells ring gloriously, and the monks begin to sing. In English. Because I sit (as inconspicuously as I can) in the back row of the balcony, I cannot see them. I only sit and listen. Sext, I have learned moments before, is prayer to renew the fervor with which one begins the day. My lost cross, I discovered, was waiting for me in the Scripture: "I am crucified with Christ: nevertheless I live; yet not I, but Christ liveth in me" (Galatians 2:20). Now, sitting before this notebook, finding my thoughts as I write them, I wonder. Have I the courage to pick it up?

None, 2:15 pm. None is a petition for strength to persevere in the day's work. Like Sext, it begins, "O God, come to my assistance." The work that I am here to do, write about Thomas Merton, seems oddly unimportant in this place.

Yesterday I felt as if I were coming to see Merton, I so identified Gethsemani with his life. Today he has fallen into the anonymity he desired. I am suddenly aware the only work worth doing is willing God's will. Marvelous paradox! To work at receiving grace, at becoming a person in whom God speaks to God.

Vespers, 5:30 pm. I sit freezing in a wool sweater and flannel shirt while the masculine strength of the monks' voices fills the church with praise. As the light fades, the Light remains present. My imagination is stirred in a wholly natural way—but more than my imagination is at work.

Christ is present.

God in Christ has already done everything. I needn't worry about walking with Christ, as if it were something I could do. I need only sit down in His grace, be still and listen. What will He tell me? The same thing He told Moses: "I AM THAT I AM" (Exodus 3:14). He will reveal Himself, not things about Himself, and I will never want to move away.

Compline, 7:30 pm. The twenty minutes of kneeling through the night office are minutes in which the Timeless inhabits time. Eternity is now. I am out of words. The ineffable has taken them as He has taken the noise I have carried all my anxious, fretful life. "We will not fear the terror by night, nor the arrow that flieth by noonday. . . . We have seen your salvation, O Lord!"

It is possible to live in Christ, in His peace and His grace. It is possible to be aware that in Him we live and move and have our being. And that in Him, through His perfected humanity which is continued in His Church, we are taken up into the life of the Trinity.

Epilogue, Oct. 14, 1977. My time here has been redemptive. My understanding of this place has deepened, as has my understanding of myself. I am called to images, to seeing through them the Christ who is the creator of all images. I am called to marriage, to living out the metaphor of the incarnation in the realities of my daily tasks. I am called to living among friends and to teaching students, to seeing in them the Christ who redeems all. And I am called not to silence, but to the silences between words that make the rhythms of poetry. I am called to the way of Affirmation.

Nearly twenty-five years passed between that Saturday afternoon, when I was a twelve-year-old boy folding bulletins at Beulah Presbyterian Church announcing my intention to be a minister, and that bright evening at the Abbey of Gethsemani when I was freed to be what God called me to be. Let me fill in some of the interval, tracing the crooked line through time.

That line took its first twist at puberty. My voice did not change. It cracked. Off and on for years. Always at the worst times. And I discovered

I had a body for which I had no imaginable use. With that body came guilt—no clear guilt related to any particular action, but just a vague, ambiguous sense of confused identity. I had no idea who I was, and my self-definition as the boy who would be a minister failed to shore up the disintegration. Peer pressure compounded the confusion.

When I left home to attend a prep school for boys, I learned I was good at only one subject: English. I could write stories, but I could not do well on exams and I could not understand grammar. In my best subject I muddled along at the rear of the advanced class.

Out of necessity I became an athlete. It was either that or suffer the ignominy of being a reject. Since I was still a runt, I joined the wrestling team. Over the next three years I grew from the lightest weight class to a respectable middle-weight class and earned a league championship. I learned to wear my collar turned up, to walk with a swagger and to sit in the smoking section of the movie theater (though "in training" I didn't smoke). I also learned to be a fake.

The most important thing I learned, I learned in the privacy of my room the night I won my league championship. I wrote a poem describing the fear I'd felt as I stood alone on the mat—knowing I'd won the championship, waiting for the referee to raise my arm signifying a victory that felt as empty and hollow as a defeat. For the first time in my life, as I wrote that poem, I made contact with my deepest self. I learned that words matter, that words are the way to truth. And I realized that I wanted, needed, to follow the way of words.

But I did not understand (and had no one to tell me) that words are tied by the incarnation of Christ to the Word. The two in my imagination became opposed. I could become a writer or I could become a minister. I could serve myself or I could serve God.

In that state of mind I went off to college. My freshman year I was devout. In the atmosphere of a more or less secular institution I held to faith. I participated in the life of a local church and through the campus ministry program I did some lay preaching in small rural churches. With a group of fellow Christians I edited a small literary magazine designed to serve as a witness. Any stories and poems I wrote were subordinate to our evangelistic cause, and it seemed to me that art fit easily into a life of Christian service. At the end of the year, convinced that my vocation was in the ministry, I transferred to an evangelical college.

There I quickly lost whatever sense of sureness I'd felt about my calling. I found myself within a community that defined commitment as conforming to the norms of a narrowly defined Christian life. Though devotional poetry fit within those norms, what I labored to write did not. Branded an outsider, I became an outsider. I began to attend, when I attended church at all, an Episcopal cathedral, and I began to read, simply because he was a Catholic and not an evangelical, Thomas Merton.

A few months later I discovered Merton's essay "Poetry and the Contemplative Life." Reading it I thought I was reading about myself.

When Thomas Merton entered Our Lady of Gethsemani in December 1941, he assumed that along with his name he would leave his poetry behind. For a time he did. But in 1943 Robert Lax, an old friend from their undergraduate days at Columbia, visited him. When he left he took with him the manuscript of *Thirty Poems*, which New Directions issued in late 1944.

Merton responded to the publication with indifference; as far as he was concerned, more poems were out of the question. Lax returned for a Christmas visit, urging him to write. Merton records his reaction to Lax's enthusiasm in *The Seven Storey Mountain* and links it to an incident shortly after:

> I did not argue about it. But in my own heart I did not think it was God's will. And Dom Vital, my confessor, did not think so either. Then one day—the Feast of the Conversion of St. Paul, 1945—I went to Father Abbot for direction, and without my ever thinking of the subject or mentioning it, he suddenly said to me, "I want you to go on writing poems."

To adequately comprehend the force of this direction, which struck Merton almost like a blow, one must understand that he was then committed to what the early church called the *via negativa* or the Way of Rejection. This way, in Charles Williams's words, "consists in the renunciation of all images except the final one of God himself." The order to continue writing poems meant to Merton the postponement of his deepest desire, which he described as "the voiding and emptying of the soul, cleansing it of all images, all likenesses that it may be clean and pure to receive the obscure light of God's own Presence."

Nevertheless Merton accepted the direction and continued to write poems. His vow of obedience left him no other choice. Unfortunately, while it ensured the production of poems, the vow could not resolve the tension Merton felt between his religious and poetic selves. He revealed the seriousness of the tension in *The Seven Storey Mountain:*

> There was this shadow, this double, this writer who followed me into the cloister. . . . I cannot lose him. He still wears the name of Thomas Merton. Is it the name of an enemy? He is supposed to be dead.
>
> He kneels with me behind the pillar, the Judas, and talks to me all the time in my ear. . . . And the worst of it is, he has my superiors on his side. They won't kick him out. . . .
>
> Nobody seems to understand that one of us has to die.

Merton's conviction that writing would destroy his spiritual life, however, was a conviction that he eventually revised and then in practice rejected. What Merton's superiors recognized from the beginning, Merton learned slowly. In *No Man Is an Island* he effectively explains why he could not give up his poetry: "Nothing that we consider evil can be offered to God in sacrifice. We give him the best that we have, in order to declare that he is infinitely better. We give him all that we prize, in order to assure him that he is more to us than our 'all.'"

Once Merton ceased to think of his poetry as an evil to be left behind, he began to understand it as a good not to be rejected but rather offered to the Lord. This led Merton to an appreciation of the Way of Affirmation. The Way of Affirmation, like the Way of Rejection, has as its end the loss of the believer in God. The means of achieving that end, however, involves looking closely at and then through the world which, as the psalms tell us, reveals the glory of God. That way is firmly established and made plain in the incarnation.

For most Christians the Way of Affirmation is the dominant way. It is the way of marriage, the way of art, the way of politics, the way of economics. It is, in short, the way of doing all things to the glory of God. It is also a dangerous way, for the things of this world can become interesting in themselves, and the wise Christian usually tempers affirmation with selected rejections. The normal Christian way, then, can be viewed as a balancing of the two mystical ways.

But the life of Thomas Merton was not that of an ordinary Christian. Both his monastic vows and his priestly orders ruled out the simple balancing act of the layperson. *The Seven Storey Mountain,* as well as the numerous recollections published since his death by his friends, shows Merton to have been incapable of doing anything halfway. Edward Rice in *The Man in the Sycamore Tree,* a popular biography he appropriately subtitles *An Entertainment,* describes his first encounter with the pre-conversion Merton at Columbia University:

> One day, after I first began to submit drawings to *Jester,* amid all the confusion of the fourth floor, I heard an incredible, noisy, barrel-house blues piano drowning out everything else (my first impression of Merton was that he was the noisiest bastard I had ever met), like four men playing at once. "Who is that crowd playing the piano?" I asked. "Only Merton," said Gene Williams. Merton soon came bustling into *Jester.* He was always full of energy and seemed unchanged from day to day, cracking jokes, denouncing the Fascists, squares, being violently active, writing, drawing, involved in everything. . . . Noisy. Authoritative. Sure of himself. But behind it all was that relentless, restless search to learn who he was.

After his conversion, Merton carried this exuberance into his spiritual life, where it became a factor in his decision to enter Gethsemani rather than joining Catherine de Heuck Doherty in her work at Friendship House, Harlem. Interestingly, as he made his choice (recorded in the last entry of *The Secular Journal of Thomas Merton*), writing seemed to be on his mind:

> Today I think: should I be going to Harlem, or to the Trappists? Why doesn't this idea of the Trappists leave me? . . . I would have to renounce more in entering the Trappists. That would be one place where I would have to give up everything. . . . Perhaps I cling to my independence, to the chance to write. . . . It seems monstrous at the moment that I should consider my writing important enough to enter into the question. . . . I return to the idea again and again: "Give up everything, give up everything!"

An appealing romanticism was involved, an excitement in going the whole route that his personality couldn't resist. But in seeing the Way of Rejection as a challenge worthy of his whole life, he also held on to a false self—an image of himself poor and sporting the tonsured haircut of a humble monk—and then involved that false self in making his choice. He would assign the values to what he would give up, and he would give up what he considered worthless to gain the experience of God he wanted. As a result he contemptuously turned his back on the world.

Merton's early journals from the monastery are filled with references to giving up writing, and it is clear that had his circumstances not been altered, he probably would have sacrificed his art. In 1948, however, his abbot died, and the order's vicar general traveled to Gethsemani for the funeral and the election of a new abbot. Merton served as his interpreter and secretary. Consequently, when Dom Gabriel Sortais was called to Louisville, Merton accompanied him, leaving the monastery for the first time in seven years. He recounts it in *The Sign of Jonas:*

> I met the world and I found it no longer so wicked after all. Perhaps the things I had resented about the world when I left it were defects of my own that I had projected upon it. Now, on the contrary, I found that everything stirred me with a deep and mute sense of compassion. I went through the city, realizing for the first time in my life how good are the people in the world and how much value they have in the sight of God.

In the course of six hours, Merton's life had been turned around. He had left the monastery committed to rejecting all images except the final one of God himself. He returned affirming, for the first time, the image called Man and seeing through that image the presence and grace of the Creator of all images. The possibility of a dual calling to poetry and to contemplation opened up to him. He responded by going forward. A year later, in *The Sign of Jonas*, he wrote, "And yet it seems to me that writing, far from being an obstacle to spiritual perfection in my own life, has become one of the conditions on which my perfection will depend."

The conflict that had tormented Merton for seven years could not be laid aside in one dramatic affirmation. His doubts recurred, but he continued to write by choice. And as he gave up his largely selfish desire to be totally absorbed in contemplation, as he willed instead God's will, he found that the inner war between his religious and poetic vocations quieted—not because he had resolved them in theory but because God had willed them reconciled in practice.

When Merton struggled to comprehend the nature of his dual calling to contemplation and poetry, he had a spiritual tradition to frame the terms of his conflict, and he had superiors to whom he owed obedience to give him direction. When I faced a similar conflict between my desire to write and my perceived "calling" to ministry, I had neither a tradition that could comprehend an artistic vocation nor a spiritual leader to whom I could turn. In confusion I dropped out of college and began to work as a laborer. I wanted to buy time and think. But in 1964 only failures left school, and I felt constant pressure to get my life back in order so that I could return to the straight and narrow road to Christian service on which I'd started out.

I remember most clearly an encounter with the minister of the church my family was then attending. I idolized him. He was an eloquent and perceptive preacher. I typed out a group of my poems, sent them to him and made an appointment to talk with him about vocation. We met one evening in his office. After about an hour of good talk, he rose to bring our session to a close. I resisted and asked about the poems. "Young man," he said, "it's time for you to put that nonsense behind you and get on with what's important in your life."

I went out in silence and closed behind me a door I never again went through. In the strangest possible way, writing the crookedest line imaginable, God had fixed my vocation; for when I closed that door, I closed it with a cold determination to go without approval, to be an artist and not a minister.

I was not, however, content. Though my act of rebellion could determine my vocation and set me on the right path, it could not form the basis for that vocation. I had to learn that another way. I turned back to Merton. With greater intellectual maturity, I understood that the difficult struggle to accept a dual vocation he wrote about in "Poetry and the Contemplative Life" was nothing like my struggle. Merton was fighting against his past, a past in which poetry represented to him the false values of fame and ambition. My struggle instead was like the hidden struggle Merton's superiors had recognized lurking behind his words: an inability to accept the worth of what my deepest self knew to be its need, the making of poems. Desperate for approval, my false self had latched on to the "ministry" course that had brought me the strongest and quickest approval I'd ever felt.

I did not understand these distinctions when I walked into the Abbey of Gethsemani that fall in 1977. But I learned them there. In *Conjectures of a Guilty Bystander,* one of his last books, Merton wrote, "A personal crisis occurs when one becomes aware of apparently irreconcilable opposites in oneself. . . . A personal crisis is creative and salutary if one can accept the conflict and restore unity on a higher level, incorporating the opposed elements in a higher unity." What I learned was that the self I had to reject was not the poem-making self that brought me disapproval but the praise-seeking self that would have used the ministry to gratify its basest desire.

Part Two

Sabbatical Journal

Sabbatical Journal

ONE

Free from teaching on sabbatical, I have a head full of projects. A day does not pass that I do not examine my progress. "How much have I written?" I ask myself. "Where am I on my reading list?" Since I am working alone with no taskmaster other than myself, I want to be sure I do more work than I would for anyone else. I want to prove to myself I'm a driver, an achiever.

It is all very foolish.

I know better. I wrote my sabbatical proposal to minimize such nonsense. Still I fall into it.

I need to remind myself writing poetry is not a career to be managed, a career to be pursued and brought to appropriate successes. It is rather a vocation, a calling and a discipline. As such, it does not lead to success. It leads to an involvement—a lived, living relationship with the world. It is an immersion, a baptism, a dying to self. It requires a renunciation of success. It requires faithfulness in the face of all obstacles.

Nothing more. Nothing less.

TWO

My cabin here on Remnant Acres is finished—more or less. As I sit at the table writing, I can see a few cracks to be sealed before the cold weather hits. And I must put a sealer on the exterior. But those are small tasks to be done later.

Linda was surprised when I brought her to see my work. She had no idea that the tongue-and-groove paneling salvaged when the college tore down Woolsey Hall would combine so well with this old Scamper pop-up I bought from Lloyd Wilt to make a permanent hideaway for me. I'm more than pleased. I look out one set of windows into a hemlock grove.

Because they are mature, I can see deep into the woods beneath them, and when inspiration fails me, I can walk about under them wondering about the kinds of fungi that thrive in their shade. A few minutes ago, I was walking under them, stepping over fallen branches, enjoying the naturalness of the restorative decay taking place. This woods is no scoured park! About one hundred yards from the cabin I stepped onto instead of over the trunk of a hemlock fallen years ago. My foot sank into it and flattened it to the ground. Amazed, I stepped onto it at another spot. The same thing happened. The whole log, still perfectly shaped, had softened to a crumbly near-humus. The forest mulches itself and thrives.

From my other windows I look into an impenetrable thicket of young poplars overgrown with raspberry canes, sumacs and some kind of clinging vine that winds through it all. When I cleared the meadow two years ago, I ran out of time before I got to it. Last year I used the cabin as a mouse-infested toolshed. I put off clearing the brush to keep the cabin hidden from the road. This year when I was scything the meadow, I kicked a large doe from the cover nearly every morning. Her regular appearance settled the fate of the thicket. It will not be cleared by me. I'm keeping other margins for wildlife; one more will not hurt any plans I have for these woods.

THREE

It rained last night; this morning is cold, and the cabin is as damp as the outdoors. The gray light of the sky hardly reaches under the trees to enter the windows. My hands are in shadow as I type. But that is all right. My whole life is in shadow as I type, for Saturday we received stunning news: the New York State nuclear siting commission has located three of its final five potential dump sites in Allegany County. To see one of them all I have to do is walk to the edge of my woods and gaze southeast across the valley.

The possibility of the dump so near—the possibility of a dump anywhere—makes the work I do here, both writing and laboring to renew the woods, increasingly important. Almost everyone's attention is turned to protest. I will be meeting with others on Saturday morning to plan civil disobedience to disrupt the surveying of specific sites. But I want to hold back. I want to resist the idea that our only recourse is protest. Protest, of course, is part of a response. But to protest is to stand against. And that is not enough. To be effective we must stand for something.

For me the work I do here is representative of what I stand for. Some days I despair. I have spent the better part of three summers working to restore the clear cut—what I call my meadow. I have worked with scythe, shovel and maddock, sweating in the sun, enduring the briars tearing at my arms, to correct the destruction it took one man an afternoon to make with a bulldozer. The futility of my resistance is almost comic. It is comic. Don Quixote.

But that is only one way of looking at it. Even alone, I am not helpless; I am a counter, one who counts for something, a representative of an alternative that can reasonably be chosen by others. In my faithfulness I live out my calling to be a steward, and in my faithfulness I invite my neighbors to join me. Enough neighbors standing together for a way of life make a neighborhood. Neighborhoods standing together make a nation.

FOUR

I went Saturday morning to the Allegany County Nonviolent Action Group (ACNAG) meeting in Belfast and spent the rest of the weekend in a deep depression. In the abstract, civil disobedience seems so easy. Now that the time has come, I am devastated, for taking this action means I have given up hope in more conventional action. It means that my trust in my state government has reached the point where I do not believe that they honestly intend to act for the good of the citizens. I believe rather that they intend to act for the benefit of the rich and powerful at the expense of the powerless and poor, at the expense of the earth, at the expense of the future.

More than that, however, contributed to my depression. I do not believe that ACNAG has sufficient direction to be effective. Throughout this whole ordeal, beginning last January, I have watched a county leadership more in love with its rhetoric of the underdog against the superpower than with results. The powers we battle love us. We scream to the newspaper, "Unjust!" and they go on in their corridors of anonymity making decisions and laughing at our innocence.

We have wasted too much time strutting when we should have been laying a foundation of legal challenge. Noncooperation at this point—holding up the drilling rigs a few days—is pointless. The decision made to come here was made in spite of and in ignorance of the facts the commission has made so much of. The next decision will be made the same way.

In frustration I write in circles. What I am struggling toward is a broken affirmation, an affirmation I have made out of idealism that I must now make in painful knowledge. The conflict between good and evil, finally, is met in the small acts of our daily lives. Staying at my desk writing my poems or cutting the bottom out of a can, flattening it and setting it aside to be recycled are more significant acts than locking arms around a bulldozer or waving a sign in front of a TV reporter. They are more significant acts because they are done for eternity. They cannot be undone. The bulldozer can be stopped, but it can be started; it will be started once my back is turned, if not here, somewhere else.

The question remains: Do I stand with ACNAG? Do I spend my time to identify with my neighbors in this struggle, engaging in an action I doubt? Or do I stand alone here in my woods putting words on paper, planting trees and trusting in an unforeseeable future?

My feeling at the moment can be summed up in the words of Robert Frost: "Me for the woods."

Perhaps what I'm struggling with here is only the writer's necessity to stand outside and observe. To enter the action is to forfeit the ability to reflect, for events move faster than thought. Nothing seems to be considered. Everything seems to be reflex, response. I am convinced, however, of one thing: writing is action. A history written on this hill has value.

FIVE

Though the routine of coming here every morning is well established, the transition I must make from business and from prose to poetry is not. The pool of drafts I rely on to get started is used up. I have no half-written poems, so each day means a new struggle to find the poem in my experience.

If I could leap out into imagination, perhaps I could find a new voice. But the habit of mind I have trained myself in does not work that way. I have come to depend on a close connection to the daily, to the ordinary, and to saying that ordinariness in my words. That I know is a limiting thing. It keeps me tied. But it is also a liberating thing. Maybe *liberating* is the wrong word. Maybe what it does is give me security. No, that's wrong too.

Authenticating? I make it a practice to say nothing in my poems I don't say in my life. I don't invent. I record and testify. In that is an aesthetic, an affirmation of a relationship between language and truth that is direct and simple.

Oh, I am aware that the heart is devious and that truth is complex, that language is subtle and can be read for secret revelations obscure even to the writer. My response is this: So too with the critic. His heart is devious and he reads with intent unknown to himself when he is functioning as writer. If the depths are past finding out, there is value in an examination of surfaces. Surfaces have their own truths. Reading them, as any canoeist knows, one reads the depths.

Behind this is a distrust of the kind of self-consciousness that assumes appearances are always false and all agendas are hidden. That I think may have been one of the causes of the fall in the garden. (Certainly it is one of the results.) Adam and Eve succumbed to the serpent's subtlety— "God didn't really mean what he said. He meant something hidden that you have to figure out. All this about not eating is really a chance for you to show initiative. God really wants you to be like himself. He said what he did so you can choose to be like him." The first deconstructionist in literary history? Nothing new under the sun?

To be a radical is not to be up to date or innovating. To be radical is to go for the root, the source. The only literary radicals left are the conservatives, the storytellers who go on from day to day unperturbed and unaffected by the winds of fashion and the imperative to change.

Is this my manifesto from the woods? Perhaps.

Simple poems, then. Poems that can be traced to life, to particulars. Poems that take thought. Poems about things.

SIX

I wrote very little yesterday. I roughed out the notes for a book review I must finish before heading west to read poems at a conference and to visit friends. It is a book review I've lost taste for. And I finished Buechner's *Brendan,* one of the books on my reading list. After that I worked in the woods.

I cleared around the huge maple butt I've been working at for several summers and found a section I'd forgotten was there. I cut it up and split most of it. When I'm done it will make about a face cord. The large section, still untouched, should make two more easily—maybe three. And I worked on the trails, cutting some more of the meadow and then leveling a section across a side hill beyond the old orchard.

Then I went fishing.

I got one bass about 12 inches and a couple of rock bass from the Genesee near Houghton.

All in all, a good day.

SEVEN

At the ACNAG meeting Saturday an air of excitement, a sense of impending action, energized everyone. Nearly a week has passed and no call for gathering has been sounded. The news, in fact, has been dull. The commissioners have designated representatives to negotiate with landowners. They in turn have been making phone calls and visits seeking permission to study the sites. And the landowners have been pretty consistently refusing. At the moment, there is nothing to do.

That brings to my mind Walter Wangerin's fantasies, *The Book of the Dun Cow* and *The Book of Sorrows*. In those books Chanticleer rules the animals. He keeps order by crowing the canonical hours. On occasion he keeps order by strapping on his fighting spurs and taking direct action to defend his kingdom. The direct action, however, seems less important than the crowing—the poetry. In *The Book of Sorrows,* after Chanticleer and the animals have defeated Wurm, Chanticleer grows broody. He is angry that it was not his action that saved the kingdom, and he seeks "something to do." He withdraws, turns his crows to formalities and perversely twists his righteous opposition to Wurm into a personal vendetta, a quarrel in which he seeks vindication. That is what Wurm wants, and that is what almost allows Wurm to win. It costs Chanticleer his life.

This story has much to say to me about my opposition to the dump. Action is necessary, but action is also a temptation. Wisdom must discern the circumstances.

I know that I am a contentious person, that I like my own way and that I am delighted when I can claim God as *my* ally. And there is the rub: God as my ally. When I enlist God, he goes AWOL and leaves me to do battle alone. I am afraid that is what I do most of the time. What I am afraid of is offering myself for service and being sent, not to the front lines and glory, but to the rear to wash pots and cook oatmeal.

Did Chanticleer come to regard his chants as making oatmeal? I think so. His animals, though they often wondered at the beauty of his crows, expected them from him. They comforted and aroused them, but Chanticleer recognized that they stirred in them no admiration. Deeds, combat, did that.

Every time I sit down here to write I come to this same point. Every day I need to do it again. Poems. Faithfulness. What sticks in my craw is my need to imagine myself as a fighter.

I lack courage, courage to be rather than do.

EIGHT

Remember.

Poetry and memory.

So often I've relied on memory. I've held it in my hand and turned it round and round like a stone. It's had a coolness and a weight I've enjoyed, treasured.

Frederick Buechner writes,

> The past and the future. Memory and expectation. Remember and hope. Remember and wait. Wait for him whose face we all of us know because somewhere in the past we have fairly seen it, whose life we all of us thirst for because somewhere in the past we have seen it lived, have maybe even had moments of living it ourselves. Remember Him who Himself remembers us as He promised to remember the thief who died beside Him. To have faith is to remember and wait, and to wait in hope is to have what we hope for already begin to come true in us through our hoping. Praise Him.

That's good writing. And I like what it says, but lately it doesn't work. And I am troubled. A couple of weeks ago in Pittsburgh, Linda was going through boxes of photographs taken when we were teenagers or younger. She kept calling me to come and see. When she called, I mostly went. But the evening was painful. I hated seeing those images of myself, of the people and places I've left behind. And I think it was painful for reasons more profound than embarrassment at an incompetent adolescence. Was it guilt for leaving them so easily? For not caring that some have been broken? For not wanting to know about the others? Maybe.

Perhaps also it is guilt for the aloneness that I have come to. I let so little touch me. Since resigning as department head at the college, I have dropped out, seeking my own peace. At times I fear what I have found is my implacability, my ability to not give a damn. Coming here to my cabin, I embrace a nonhuman world. The trees are enough for me. There is almost no one in the valley I really care to see. Oh, I go about being social. That is easy now that I don't let anyone into my aloneness. It's so easy to avoid risk and hurt.

Am I hard on myself? I hope so. But my disconnectedness is a kind of hopelessness. I'm not sitting here waiting for anything or anyone. Or am I? Didn't Eliot say something about waiting without hope, for hoping would be hoping for the wrong thing? If so, I've got it down.

I'm waiting for a poem. I've got three months with nothing to do but write poems, and I haven't got an idea in my head.

Well.

I remember.

I remember my sins, my ego, my foolishness, and I haven't the courage to make poems of them. I haven't the nerve to let anyone see as deeply into me as writing the only poems I have left to write would show. So I hide. Brother Jack, the Hidden.

Could it be that at this moment in my life, when the skill I've labored to develop, when the opportunities I've sought, when the time is mine, I no longer have the courage or desire to write? I want to retreat from the very thing I have lived my life for and disappear?

Remember.

I don't want to remember. I want to forget.

Hope.

I don't want to hope. Hope requires faithfulness, working in the dark without results, and I'm tired.

So I go forward using what I've completed as if it's new. *Hoping*—I was going to write *hoping*. Without thinking, I was going to say *hoping*. So perhaps I do hope. Perhaps I do wait. But what for? Right now for something as simple as a poem that does not hurt too much to write. A beginning.

I would like to abandon being here and being known. I would like to go off where I could live without my past, where I could bury it all and be reborn. Then I could have this slow dying done with. Then I could quit babbling to give myself a sense of working.

NINE

Through May, June and July I wrote easily, often falling back on memory—usually falling back on memory. I finished a sequence of poems I called "Leax Lane" after the place where I lived the early years of my life in the midst of an extended intergenerational family. In the sequence I chronicled the post-World War II transition of my family from a family of farmers to a family of dispersed, suburban white-collar workers. As I was completing it I worked on another group of poems tying the present to the past, linking, making connections.

Then in August I had a dream about my father that I turned into a poem:

> My father was with me.
> In my new car, an Escort wagon,
> we turned up Brown Avenue
> out of Turtle Creek and headed home
> to Leax Lane.
>
> The engine, running like a dream,
> purred as we sped past Sunday drivers.
> Cruising the long straight-a-way
> from Bill Free's, where my father worked,
> to the White Horse Inn, where I played
> pinball with Butch, I asked,
> "Do you think we might get
> some fishing in this summer?"
> "A couple days," my father said.
> "We can go up the river."
>
> Then we reached Leax Lane.
> All the mailboxes were shiny new.
> Aunt Dot's had nothing in it.
> Ours bore someone else's name.
>
> I didn't notice until later
> that Baker's barn was gone.
> Starting up the lane, the car
> lost power. I downshifted
> and lurched forward, but halfway

up the hill in front of Mrs. Lackatoss's
house the engine died.

"Something wrong?" my father asked.
"The car," I said,
"I can't get up the lane."

Angry, I got out. Grasping the front
bumper, as if I grasped the bridle
of a balking horse, I pulled.
"Come on," I cried. "Move."
Then from his seat my father
gently spoke. "I'm sorry,"
he said. "You seem to have
forgotten. I'm dead.
The lane is closed."

Writing those words ended my fluency. When I finished the poem, I thought I was saying that the past cannot be re-created, or at least can be (re)created only fictively. After this morning's outburst of prose, however, I suspect that the dream meant something more frightening.

The lane is closed, not because it is in the past but because I've been trying to use it without keeping it alive in the present. The past is not usable; that is, it cannot be used.

The past is not usable, that is, it cannot be used merely as material without being used up. Only a living relationship keeps providing substance. A mine is played out; a garden goes on forever when tended.

I must face the truth. No Leaxes live on Leax Lane anymore. They are all dead or gone. And I have not written, visited or talked with any of the living for two or three years—maybe longer. By that withdrawal of myself I have closed the lane to myself.

Can I, the prodigal, talk about love? Talk about caring? Talk about reverence?

Talk about reverence? Not without a deep ambivalence. The best my poems manage is to live in a fictive world that hides what memory brings forth in what false imagination desires it to be.

I think the poems I've written have been connected. Through most of my life, I was connected. I visited often enough to remain a part of things. But my father died. Then as Grandma faded into helpless senility and my aunts became widows, it all became too difficult. Every visit plunged me back into a swirling storm of emotion I did not want to endure. Am I looking for an excuse? I hope not. I think I'm merely trying to understand what happened.

But I'm not sure I'm getting anywhere. I wonder if I'm creating a crisis to account for simple sloth. I don't much want to write poems.

TEN

After two weeks traveling and a week reestablishing routine, I return to thought. The dump has been out of my mind, at least as a particular problem. The dump as the presence of the destruction of the earth, however, traveled with me. It is ever present. And so, consequently, is the nagging question of how I live my life in opposition to such destruction.

On my travels and this past week, I reread *Confessions of a Rebel* and *Marriage of a Rebel,* the two volumes of autobiography by the deaf-blind Cornish poet Jack Clemo. I am sympathetic to his erotic quest, to his identification of marriage as a key mystical experience. But I have great difficulty with his theology of the fall which sunders the natural from the supernatural—indeed opposes the two. The earth, he argues, is corrupt. There is nothing in nature except deception. Life grows out of death—the more death (compost) the more life. And he recoils. The same follows for marriage. Only Christian marriage, somehow mystically transformed, does not participate in the perverse drive to fecundity of the Life Force.

His error, made plain in his theological tract *The Invading Gospel,* is a dualism that opposes Christ and Satan as equally independent though unequally matched contestants for souls. Following from this he aligns nature with Satan and rejects it.

The fall, however, did not do that. The corruption of nature by humanity's sin did not result in a fallen biology, did not result in parasites and carnivores. They were there all along with the masticating herbivores. Everything ate something. Fruit ripened and fell in the garden. And Adam shat in the bushes and planted seeds.

What happened at the fall and what causes the earth to cry out for the day of redemption is that Adam broke his relationship not only to God but to God's creation.

Now earth suffers human abuse. There is nothing evil in a storm or a flood (as Clemo asserts). What is evil is the insistence on controlling storms and floods. The refusal to get one's butt out of the flood plain. Because humans have made their will and convenience the measure of the earth's goodness, they have assigned an evil that is not there to the creation. (I realize that I am omitting the problem of diseases, cancers, strokes, hardened arteries, birth defects, etc. Much of that I suspect can be dealt with in terms of the consequences of sin—many diseases resulting from the pollution of the environment and/or personal sin. But I am looking at the core attitude and relational stance that defines how one approaches the earth.)

If the creation is not good, there is no valid revelation, for all revelation comes into creation and speaks the language of creation. Christ spoke in parables, and his parables were stories of an agricultural people. He spoke of birth and death. What else could he speak of?

So that is what I speak of. My life is the life of a village storyteller. I tell the stories of the people I live among. I tell stories to the people I live among.

That is my role. That is my calling. But I also live a story I have chosen.

That story is the story of the fall and the redemption. I am fallen for I have acted out in my life the life of Adam. Here is what I mean. I don't believe anyone inherits damnation. I believe one gets it the old-fashioned way; one earns it. Original sin, however, cannot be dismissed. I do not believe that human nature is essentially good or that humans can save themselves. What seems to be true to experience is that everyone personally reenacts the fall. What we inherit from Adam is a world so distorted by the choices of our ancestors that we inevitably make our willful choice and enter into sin, disturbing the potentials of all our relationships. The entry into a relationship with Christ is an entry into restoration that is a lifelong process, a process of reclamation.

Christ in the world is a man with a shovel standing at the edge of a strip mine. In his imagination he remembers the contours of the hill. And as he begins the apparently impossible task, he knows that he will succeed. But he also knows that the coal has been burned. What was once can never be again. Loss is part of the story forever. But what can be remains to become.

That is our task. Here and hereafter. Our redemption is the redemption of the earth. The two cannot be separated.

ELEVEN

I've come back to the cabin to write letters, thank-you notes and overdue epistles to friends I haven't seen in ages. But my self-absorption pushes me to these pages. I wonder what I'm doing here almost every day, scribbling pages that will never be seen. Do I secretly hope that my mind, my insistent worrying of a few themes, will become a classic journal? Why else do I stay at it except for vanity?

Surely that is a part of it, the least attractive part. But surely there is something else. I read through all these pages this morning, and I felt as if I had been writing to someone I wanted to know me, someone I wanted to help me. I don't know who. If I did I'd probably write him/her a letter. Strange. I have friends. I'm writing this instead of a letter. And I have Linda. We talk. I don't consciously hide from her. Yet I know I'm always hiding. Even this morning as I walked back to the car after writing and thinking about how memory has closed to me, I knew that part of the reason memory has closed is I have no way of coming out with what is left. What is left is for prayer—not for confession. In this age, it's easy to name sins. It's the fashion. But the deep wounds, the unfathomable mysteries of our persons and our relationships. How and why do we love? What is love beyond the consciously kept commitments made in darkness then lived in the glare of light?

What does it mean to be broken and made whole? What does it mean to be alone? How does being alone differ from loneliness?

How did I get to these questions? What story would I tell to explain? Dare I try?

I do.

Long ago the Genesee Canal ran through the field behind my house. It was filled, wheelbarrow load by wheelbarrow load, by two bachelors who were old men when I moved into the neighborhood. They didn't quite finish, however, and so when it rains the field fills with enough water to float a canoe. This summer we have had nothing but rain. A few mornings ago, after I emptied the compost bucket into the bin, I stooped over to rinse it in the pond spreading before me. A swirl erupted where I dipped the bucket, and a three-foot watersnake that had been hidden in the weedy shallows whipped into deeper water. I stepped back quickly, caught myself and then watched. It swam about fifteen feet from me and stopped, its relatively small head poking from the water, its heavy, diamond-marked body resting doubled on itself on the grassy bottom. Only when it swam, stretching itself out to cut eel-like through the water, was its full length clear.

To make it swim, I scooped a bucket of water and sent a shower falling over it. It ducked its head and slipped sinuously farther from me, stopped, and once again popped its head up. I heard my daughter, Melissa, at the back door, so I called her. She stood beside me, saw nothing for a moment and then gasped, "What's that thing doing down here?"

"It was right at the edge of the water. I scared it when I dumped the compost."

"I'm glad it was you," she said and stepped back from the water.

We stood together watching it. It hung limp and lazy in the water. I pitched another bucket's worth at it, causing it to speed off another five or six yards, but it seemed content to lounge where it was, and we left it.

As we walked away, I thought about how easy it is to admire the lithe strength and sudden quickness of a snake, how easy it is to be fascinated from a distance, and yet how hard it is to feel anything but fear and anxiety close to one. I think that fear and anxiety is learned. I learned it before I was five years old; while still living at Leax Lane, I stepped barefooted on a coiled blacksnake. Forty years later I cannot help leaping backwards when I come upon even a small one. My little sister learned it with age. Because my brother grew up wanting to be a herpetologist, we had snakes as pets. I remember my sister, as a child, allowing a grass snake to curl around her arm and crawl inside her shirt.

"Look, Mom," she said, laughing.

My mother looked, then fled. My sister, now grown and a mother herself, remembers the moment with awe and disbelief.

Genesis tells us the animosity humans feel for snakes comes from Satan's taking the form of a serpent to beguile and then weave his deception on Eve. It also tells us the snake's peculiar, fascinating slither on its belly is God's punishment for that deception. As a naturalist I don't quite know what to do with Genesis, but as a reader and observer I know in myself the power of the passage. I know the way the story has affected my perceptions and the way my perceptions have enlivened the story. Though I know how snakes fit in the ecology of my garden, field and woods, though I know enough to let them live, I cannot live beside them easily. I've watched a black racer stalk a mouse across the sand landscape of a cage, toss a coil about it and devour it headfirst. I've been appalled. Why I should feel such keen aversion at the coldness of the mouse's death, when watching an osprey fall from the sky to take a fish fills me with awe, I do not understand. But in this strange emotion I find myself bound with others; I cannot easily love a snake in the grass.

A snake in the grass. Curious the way we use that innocently descriptive phrase as a metaphor to characterize people we distrust. I wonder if our use comes from the suddenness with which we happen upon snakes or from our biblical association with the devil—or more particularly with the beguiling serpent who courted Eve and won her trust for evil ends. Perhaps it doesn't matter. Either way, it fits, and to call someone a snake is not a compliment.

The summer I was fifteen, while working at a church camp as a counselor-in-training, I was befriended by a man whose nickname was Snake. Mostly my job was running the camp store, keeping the kids in soda pop and ice cream. On counselors' days off, however, I would lead evening devotions in the cabins and tuck the kiddies into bed. Then I'd sit around with the real counselors and feel important. Snake was one of the senior counselors. He was probably twenty-two or twenty-three, and he had been working at the camp for years. Snake wasn't the most attractive of men. Though he was tall and relatively well proportioned, he was not athletic, and his complexion had an odd gray pallor to it that suggested he needed to wash—or, as I think now, that he needed to shed a skin. As unsavory as this description makes him appear, he was a pleasant man, good-humored to be around and well-meaning in his relationships. I trusted him not only because he was a senior counselor but because he seemed trustworthy.

One evening, late, after I had tucked some other counselor's campers into bed, I sat on a set of cabin steps with Snake, waiting for the muffled voices around us to quiet and the campers to fall asleep before we went down to the lounge. Gradually our conversation drifted to spiritual matters as Snake played the role of senior counselor, asking questions about my relationship to Jesus. At first I answered openly; I had nothing to hide, I believed in Jesus and wanted him to rule my life. But his questions became more probing, and as I became uncomfortable, I became reticent. Sensing my reticence, he pressed, "There's something bothering you. You can talk to me. Tell me what it is."

We talked for over an hour, and when we finally went down to the lounge, I'd told all my secrets—not only the ones I'd known but also others I hadn't even thought of until I told them. As I talked, I felt a wash of excitement, a tremendous emotional release. There in the dark, close to tears, sharing my life, I believed I was doing a good thing. But the next morning I woke feeling violated, as if I had yielded up a kind of virginity and granted Snake an inappropriate knowledge of my personhood. Why, apart from a taste for spiritual voyeurism, had Snake, who was little more than a stranger, wanted me to talk? No good came of it. Though he never betrayed my confidences to anyone, he had beguiled me into betraying myself. I never confided in him again.

Since that night, in fact, I've held back from everyone. I'm jealous of my self, and I step back from confidences as quickly as I step back from snakes. I know they have a place in the spiritual ecology of my life, but I like them the way I like snakes—controlled, contained behind glass or viewed from a distance.

We're between rains now. The water in the back field has receded, but when I go to the compost I'll look for the snake. I'll watch where I put my feet, and I'll keep my secrets hidden in the confines of art.

TWELVE

Two weeks ago I was wondering if I'd write again. The burden of my dream poem and weariness with repeating myself wore on me like water on sandstone. But I have come back to my cabin and my typewriter, and I have started new poems. I have a sense of the rightness of doing them. I have a sense that my life is to be lived in obedience to a calling that may keep me here or move me, and I am content either way. I think.

I also have a sense that calling is not to be confused with being a writer—one punching out the books and making a name, being read and admired. The calling has to do with sitting here and accepting silence if necessary. The silence of not writing. The silence of keeping back my poems until I have tested them in time. The silence of having the poems rejected.

The last silence is the worst, for it is never clear. It shouts "Failure!" to the part of me that wants to shine. It says, "I'm not ready for you to be heard," to the part of me that accepts the vocation. It strikes at both my best and my worst. And I cannot separate them.

THIRTEEN

A light rain has started to fall on the cabin roof—on the rest of the woods as well. It sounds much like the leaves dropping on other days, except the sound is steady. There are no sudden bangs of small sticks landing on their ends. But I am dry. In the eight weeks (actually six, since I was away for two) I have been coming here I have done nine new (wholly new—not worked-over drafts) poems. For me a tremendous output considering that when I first came up here I wondered if I would ever write another poem.

Mornings like this I wonder anew. The old guilt rides in. "Listen Buster, you're on sabbatical to write poems, so get writing." Any slowing of the movement brings panic.

Two things happen. On the one hand, I get in a groove and want to repeat myself, or at least build in a single direction. On the other hand, I want to do something radically different, to take risks and discover new things. Though the two can over the long haul fit together, my impatience can't manage the waiting act. And I go dry. I can't follow the advice William Stafford gives in his little essay "A Way of Writing." I can't patiently fish for ideas the way he does. I can't take what comes. I'm locked into a commitment. A kind of evangelism hides under my work. I have a program. That may not be bad.

In a brighter, better poet than I am, such a focus might be limiting. For myself it is perhaps the only way to make "something" of my gift. It is also a way to become bored and boring. I remember with little fondness the reviewer who described *The Task of Adam* as "a bunch of poems about the garden that grow quickly repetitious."

The rain has stopped.

FOURTEEN

I split a small stack of firewood this morning. As I worked I thought about what I wrote yesterday. More and more lately, I've been moved to think of myself as one of the middle poets—as a craftsman who can do some nice things but not one who is likely to be important or read in the future. As one content to write a good poem for a local (in place and time) audience. That local audience may be spread across the U.S., but that doesn't change its essential cultural localness. The metaphor that came to me was of a marathon. Many people run them, but few aspire to win. Most just want to finish. That is satisfaction enough.

Some days this move toward accepting myself as a "middle-man" causes me to despair. I think it's middle age. I think it's being stuck in the boonies with no connection. Other days I think it's mental health.

Still other days I think of Hopkins and Herbert, poets whose greatness was never known to them; readers discovered it after their deaths. And I hope for that.

It isn't a bad image—a faithful servant of the Lord working in obscurity (faithfully with no honor) only to be honored by the ages.

It's an evil image, one filled with romantic pride that demonstrates how far short of sainthood I am.

I wonder if Hopkins and Herbert had secret ambitions.

FIFTEEN

I often have the feeling when I write my poems that I am not writing them but that some person I will to become is doing the writing. And that if that writing is not done, I will never become that person I seek to be. This sense stands in contradiction to the other feeling I have as I write, that I can write nothing that is not rooted in my lived experience. The first idea/sense is visionary; the second is testimonial.

They come together, perhaps, when the visionary grows out of the testimonial, when the actual is the seed of what is to come. Who can see the oak in the acorn? Yet the two are one, first in potential and then in fact. Though many acorns fail to become oaks, all oaks were once acorns. That is a neat statement. No loose ends. But it is also an analogy. Does the acorn imagine itself an oak? Can it make false claims? Does it grow by that imagination? And thereby make the false claims true? Is that how a human grows?

Part Three

Becoming a New Creation

Telling Affirmations

Truth by Moonlight

Becoming a New Creation

It took a high school athletic event to dump me into poetry. For three years I had been on the wrestling team. My sophomore year I made the varsity, but I lost match after match. My junior year I sat on the sidelines with a cracked arch. My senior year, healthy and experienced, I began belatedly to win. At tournament time, February 1961, I was seeded second in my weight class. During the regular season the man who was seeded first had beaten me by a point when, thinking I had injured him, I let him go. He drew the first round bye. I wrestled six minutes. In the second round he pinned in fifty seconds. I wrestled six minutes.

We met in the finals, my third full match of the day. I won on riding time. Standing in the center of the mat waiting for the official decision and the ceremonial raising of my arm in victory, I realized that through the whole match I had been afraid and that my fear had kept me from risking enough to win decisively. Walking through the applause toward my cheering teammates, I realized not only that I was still afraid but also that my fear had no object.

That night after the celebration (we'd won five individual titles and the team championship), I sat down with a blank sheet of paper and wrote about my fear. For the first time in my life I allowed my words to make contact with my deepest feelings. The writing was difficult and painful. When I finished, I found I had written a poem. And when I read it, I found my image in my words.

Today, as a creative writing teacher in a Christian college, I am most surprised not by how few students write poetry, but by how many write poetry under exactly the same emotional circumstances that started me writing. This instinctive recognition of poetry as a way to come to terms with experience intrigues me and has led me to ask what is happening in and to a person engaged in writing a poem.

Before that February night, when I set down my first poem, I wanted to write fiction and only fiction. It is half amusing, half embarrassing, to explain why. Fiction fit my image. Hemingway was my idol. Following him, I wanted to catch big fish, shoot big animals and tell big tales. Poetry was unimaginable. Even when my friends expressed a passion for it, I wanted nothing to do with it. I think I sensed that writing it required an honesty I was unwilling to strive for, a willingness to take risks I was not up to.

But after that first glimpse of myself, that recognition of fear and my confrontation of it on the page, writing poetry became a habit. I learned to enjoy the work and exhilaration of wrestling with words and experiences. I quickly understood that the most important thing I could do was use poetry to define my life. What I did not understand was the treachery of poetry. I fell into the trap that waits at every turn. Half understanding Wordsworth, I believed in powerful feelings and in personal feelings. Belief led to introspection and terrible poems. I wrote such lines as

> Is it a madness or a god
> that comes galloping through my mind
> on steel shod hooves of raging destiny . . .

Looking at them now, I find it hard to forgive myself, but I recall T. S. Eliot's assertion that poets only have subjects every four or five years. Most of the time their writing is preparation, a kind of training for the moments of real engagement. He's right, of course. The preparation he refers to is an absolute necessity. It involves, I think, two things: verbal facility and the ability to recognize the significant subject when it appears. The two do not always come together. Though they came together for me on an elemental level on my first try, it would be several years before they came together again.

Too much romanticism and too much introspection drove me out of college midway through my junior year. Hoping to think my life clear, I took a job as a warehouseman. On my vacation I attended a church-sponsored conference for college students. The conference was typical; I had fun with my friends. The evangelist spoke well, but for the most part ineffectively—that is, his messages had little apparent effect on us.

A Communion service was scheduled for the last afternoon. Between lunch and Communion I sat on the hillside overlooking the valley and confessed to a friend that I didn't feel free to take Communion. We decided to pray. Suddenly I was overwhelmed. Tears began pouring from my eyes, and words—intelligible English words—began pouring from my mouth. I prayed as I had never prayed before.

After the Communion service, still crying, I went to the evangelist to tell him what had happened.

"Thank God, brother," he said, clapping his arm around my shoulders. "You've finally been saved."

I was too confused to protest I had been saved for ten years, and only as I later talked with friends did I come to understand the magnitude of the error that had occurred. The evangelist, however innocently, had carelessly labeled my experience, and I had accepted his label. Whatever God had intended to give me that afternoon on the hillside had been stolen from me by inappropriate language.

Two years later I tried to reconstruct that afternoon in a poem.

> that day the
> words
> formed
> not in my mind
> but on my lips
> a bird hung
> silently
> in the shy
> and the Word
> burned
> my tongue
> like a flaming
> Host
> until
> my eyes boiled

Writing helped me recapture the moment, but even so, the meaning of the experience remains obscure to me. All I have said is that some special revelation of—or visitation by—the Holy Spirit took place. Yet that much definition was sufficient to change the pattern of my poetry and my life. It led me to consider the relationship of the Holy Spirit to the creative process. I began with a favorite verse of Scripture:

Likewise the Spirit also helpeth our infirmities: for we know not what we should pray for as we ought: but the Spirit itself maketh intercession for us with groanings which cannot be uttered. (Romans 8:26)

Thinking on paper, I played with what the passage suggested:

> It is not enough
> to say simply
> anymore
>
> to say simply . . .
> anything
>
> The Spirit
> must groan
>
> white dove
> descending
> in flames

Two things quickly emerged: a controlling image and a crude structure. The image is a common one, the Spirit as a dove. It contributed little toward making the poem come alive. The structure, however, gave me something to work with. Reminiscent of the argumentative pattern of a sonnet, the opening two stanzas state a problem; the closing two stanzas suggest a resolution. It is twofold: the Spirit must speak for us, and the Spirit must fill us. While I obviously had no way of knowing it, everything that would be included in the final version of the poem was present in embryo.

My task was to write until I understood what I intuited. The first rewrite produced two major gains. I allowed the statement of the problem room to define itself more clearly, and I broke from the traditional characterization of the Spirit.

> It is not enough
> anymore
> to say simply
>
> to rely on wit
> and form
> alone
>
> The heart moves

too quickly
to be caught
in a trap of words
The Spirit must groan
plummet down
and sit
like a bird of prey
alive and fierce
on your lips

The resulting glimpse of the terrible awesomeness of the Spirit turned the poem in a direction I never expected. But it still wasn't what I was after. The image of the bird pecking on lips reminded me of Isaiah's burning coal, so I tried it. As soon as I wrote it, I knew it fit. I also knew the poem was exploding in four directions. I copied it over, altering the last stanza, but the means to explain the transformation of the words into the Word eluded me.

to say simply
anymore
is not enough
The heart moves
too quickly
to rely on wit
or form
alone

The Spirit must scream
plummet down
like a bird of prey
and sit fierce
talons clenching
your bleeding lips
so your words become
his words
and his words become
your words
and the elementary words
at last become
fused in the Word
and your speech
be resurrected
in the agony of (blood) pain
where words
become fused in the Word

A simple but profound substitution proved to be the key to completing the poem: I remembered T. S. Eliot's statement that the life of a poet is a process of continual self-extinction. I changed the lines

> in the agony
> of (blood) pain

to

> in the agony
> of self-extinction

The solution at hand, I began the hard process of cutting the waste from the poem and making it as intelligible as possible. Several difficult drafts later I finished "On Writing Poetry."

> The Spirit must scream
> plummet down
> like a bird of prey
> and sit   fierce
> talons clenched
> in your bleeding lips
>
> and your words become
> his Word
> and his Word become
> your words
> that your speech
> dead in the agony of self
> might be resurrected
> in self-extinction

At that point, I had no idea of the importance of what I had written. Much later, long after the poem was published, I discovered I had worked out something of a poetic.

Poetry for me could no longer be a matter of powerful, personal feelings. Both would enter in, but both would be subjected to a greater purpose. The poem became the field of composition, the place where my words which image me are through the power of the Holy Spirit wedded to the Word. I recognized poetry as a means of shaping myself, not into my own image as I had been doing, but as a means of finding myself being made into the image of Christ.

Before I attempt to draw conclusions from this personal account, there are two points of potential confusion that need to be clarified. The first is the concept of self-extinction. The second is the implied concept of poetic inspiration. The two are closely related.

In "Tradition and the Individual Talent," an essay to which I continually return, T. S. Eliot writes,

> Tradition is a matter of much wider significance. It cannot be inherited, and if you want it you must obtain it at great labor. . . . What is to be insisted upon is that the poet must develop or procure the consciousness of the past and that he should continue to develop this consciousness throughout his career.
>
> What happens is a continual surrender of himself as he is at the moment to something which is more valuable. The progress of an artist is a continual self-sacrifice, a continual extinction of personality.

In other words, poets who desire to compose works with meaning extending beyond the limits of their own idiosyncrasies must subject those idiosyncrasies to the discipline of tradition. If they want to live as artists, they must die as individuals.

There is a parallel in Scripture: "He that findeth his life shall lose it: and he that loseth his life for my sake shall find it" (Matthew 10:39). Just as Christians find freedom in bondage to Christ, artists find freedom in tradition. In each case the true meaning of the individual is discovered through a voluntary surrender of the self.

The issue of inspiration is more problematic. In *A Christian View of Art and Literature,* Calvin Seerveld takes issue with those who hold that art is in any special way inspired by the Holy Spirit: "Maybe a mystified ignorance led Aristotle into the trap, but it must take a stubborn or evil-minded pride ('You will be like God,' said Satan) for men today to persist in avowing that their art is the act of divine inspiration."

I agree with Seerveld. He is right in emphasizing the distinction between poetry and Scripture. But there is another way to look at the inspiration of art. As Christians we are not naturalists; we are supernaturalists. We believe in the Trinity, each member of which functions in the continual creation of the world. Christ had to leave the disciples and ascend into heaven so the Holy Spirit could come to each believer. "Nevertheless," Christ said, "I tell you the truth; it is expedient for you that I go away: for if I go not away, the Comforter will not come unto you; but if I depart, I will send him unto you" (John 16:7).

Not only does Christ send the Spirit, he sends him with power—power not only to regenerate us but power to be expressed through us. After healing the man lame from birth, Peter spoke to the crowd: "Ye men of Israel, why marvel ye at this? Or why look ye so earnestly on us, as though by our own power or holiness we had made this man to walk?" (Acts 3:12).

Since Christians, artists as well as evangelists, have within them the power of the Holy Spirit, it is only logical to conclude that artists who bring everything into captivity for Christ write—just as they live—under the direction of the Holy Spirit.

The relationship between this conception of inspiration and the poetic theory of self-extinction becomes apparent. The Holy Spirit is the agent who enables the artist to transcend the merely personal. The Spirit weds the individual artist's image to the image of Christ. We can conclude then that the process that takes place as Christian poets write is similar to that described in 2 Corinthians 3:18: "But we all, with open face beholding as in a glass the glory of the Lord, are changed into the same image from glory to glory, even as by the Spirit of the Lord."

Writing, poets come to know themselves not as alienated individuals but as creations made over into the image of Christ. Consequently their poems are not private; they are images incarnated for themselves and for the community in which they live.

Telling Affirmations

For many years I was a failed novelist, a would-be writer of fiction who after two halting efforts, one in high school and one in college, had never finished a credible story. I remember a day early in my career as a graduate student. I was taking a fiction-writing seminar and had turned in the opening twenty-five pages of a novel about a young man in love. My professor, a big, boisterous ex-navy man, looked across his desk to me with pity in his eyes.

"Here's what I want you to do," he said. "Take this stuff with you, go home, buy a bottle of bourbon, drink half of it, and start over."

I must have looked at him incredulously, for he continued, "You're too tight."

I said nothing, but I wondered, "If I'm tight now, what do you suppose I'll be after half a bottle of bourbon?"

"You have to get loose," he lectured. "Get some distance from your subject. Let your characters romp and be themselves."

Ten months later, at the end of the seminar, I sat before him with fifty pages of a novel about a young man in love. By then we were friends; I'd located an army surplus store that sold navy watchcaps, and I had bought two for him. But our friendship didn't change his judgment, and I think my failure to let my characters live pained him. Sadness colored his voice as he summed up my work: "Well, you did poetry for your thesis, so I guess this doesn't matter too much."

The trouble was, it mattered a great deal, for I wanted more to be a novelist than to be a poet. I left graduate school with his pronouncement echoing in my head, and I determined to prove it wrong. He had suggested to me two methods for writing a novel. The first was to know a character, set up a situation and see what happens when that character begins to act. The second was to set up a sequence of events and move the character through them. Each way had its difficulties. The first was unpredictable. Anything could happen; a story could suddenly take on a life of its own and fly out of control. The second was predictable. Nothing unplanned could enter to disrupt the smooth march from beginning to middle to end.

Urging me to get loose, my professor had been urging me to follow method one. Free of his pressure, I determined to try method two. I outlined. I planned. I created a great chart of my novel and traced a timeline on wrapping paper tacked across the wall above my desk. I set out to follow it to completion.

Each evening after work (I was supposedly teaching Thoreau to eleventh-grade girls taking the business curriculum) I abandoned my wife, closeted myself and marched to my silent drummer. I marched for three months and then gave up. My novel, so carefully planned, was as hopeless as the sprawl I'd written in class. I knew my character as well as I knew myself, I knew everything that was supposed to happen in the unfolding of my narrative, and I knew what that narrative was supposed to mean, but I could not make it live. Finally, one day, not despairing but realizing I would never complete that novel, I took everything—my graduate school manuscript, my wrapping-paper timeline, my second draft—and burned it all. As I watched the flames I felt a wonderful sense of release.

When I moved to teaching at the college level, the busyness of my academic life swallowed up my desire to write fiction; I had fifty students in beginning composition, fifteen in a writing workshop and another dozen in a modern poetry seminar. It was all I could do to scratch out an occasional poem. One night, reading late after everyone else had gone to bed, I discovered William Faulkner had once called all novelists failed poets. I laughed to myself. I was a failed novelist slowly turning into a poet. I decided to accept Faulkner's order of value and content myself with being the better thing.

For ten years after that, I thought of fiction only when I read it. I read my way through Ernest Hemingway, John Updike, Robert Penn Warren, J. D. Salinger, Kurt Vonnegut, Reynolds Price, Edward Abbey, Wallace Stegner, Wendell Berry, Flannery O'Connor, John Steinbeck, Frederick Buechner, Walker Percy, Willam Golding and others. I read purely for enjoyment, and though I noticed the skill I paid no conscious attention to craft. Then one of my colleagues resigned, and I was assigned the fiction-writing class. Suddenly, to help my students I had to be aware of craft. I had to see fiction as a writer. I had to explain how successful stories worked and how failed stories failed. In front of my students, thinking on my feet, stumbling, I began to learn.

The first two things I learned were technical.

Aristotle's discussion of what it means for a story to have a beginning, a middle and an ending has not been superseded. A story begins with an action that has not been caused by anything before it. It develops by elaborating the consequences of that action, and it ends when those consequences have run their course. Nothing extraneous can be admitted. Only by adhering tightly to these strictures can a writer achieve closure, the sense of completeness necessary to the success of the story.

Hemingway is the contemporary master of dialogue. By his practice he taught every writer following him that dialogue is not the faithful reproduction of people talking. It is rather a fabrication that creates the illusion of people talking. Where talk is effusive, dialogue is crisp, even cryptic. It omits and by its omission implies more than it could otherwise contain. Less is more.

As important as these technical lessons were—I think fiction lives or dies by them—I had something more important to learn. I found it in an essay by Flannery O'Connor. She wrote,

> It is a good deal easier for most people to state an abstract idea than to describe and thus recreate some object that they actually see. But the world of the fiction writer is full of matter, and this is what the beginning fiction writers are loath to create. They are concerned primarily with unfleshed ideas and emotions. They are apt to be reformers and to want to write because they are possessed not by a story but by the bare bones of some abstract notion. They are conscious of problems, not of people.

When I read those words, I understood for the first time the failure of my novel and what my professor meant when he advised me to let my characters romp and be themselves. I could not let them romp, for I was unnecessarily prudish and disapproved of romping. I could not let them be themselves, for my ideas about what their lives meant interested me more than their lives. I did not understand what O'Connor would make plain later in the same essay, that "when you write fiction you are speaking *with* character and action, not *about* character and action."

Understanding this, however, only made me a critic; it did not make me a writer of fiction. A conversation and a vague sense of guilt did that. The guilt came from the old saw "If you can't, teach. If you can't teach, teach teachers." I was a self-admitted failed novelist teaching fiction writing. Though my teaching was far better than my practice had been, I could not help but feel a lack of authority for my pronouncements. I began to play with the idea of getting around to maybe doing a story or two. Then one day about six months into the writing of my prose journal, *In Season and Out,* I had lunch with Cheryl Forbes and Judith Markham, my editors for that project. As we were discussing the nature of my narrative, Cheryl casually asked, "Have you ever written fiction?"

"It was my dream once," I answered. "But it's been lost with time and busyness."

Judith looked at me, questioning. "You never think about it?"

I shrugged.

"You ought to," she said. "Maybe when you're done with this, you can do some for us."

Over the next few months, I began to think about what I expected from fiction. Why did I read it? Why would I want to write it? Though I am not a great fan of fantasy, my occasional reading of it, particularly the work of Tolkien, suggested to me an answer to the first question that is clearly supported by my enjoyment of mysteries and, I believe, ultimately supported by all fiction.

Fantasy, more than anything else, is about the eucatastrophe, the ending in which all sorrows turn to joy. Terrible things happen. Battles are won and lost. Heroes fall and die. But in the end their actions have meaning. Light divides the darkness, and hope prevails. Fantasy resonates with Christian implications. Its development affirms the pattern of the Christian story. Christ is crucified. He dies. Neither his suffering nor his death is revoked; both are real. But he rises from the dead—his resurrection redefining his suffering and making the world new.

Mysteries are about crime and justice. An ordered world is disturbed, usually by a murder. A genius—Peter Wimsey, Albert Campion or Adam Dalgliesh—enters, exercises either intellect or intuition, discovers (often through some trial or imaginative identification with the criminal) "who done it" and, without revoking the horror, restores order. Once again the pattern of the Christian story of sin, retribution and restoration is acted out.

It became clear to me that I read fiction not only for the excitement and diversion of the story but for the affirmation of meaning inherent in its pattern, its bedrock belief in an ordered world where actions have both consequences and meanings. This became problematic when I turned to the question of writing fiction. To write fiction, to shape patterns that affirmed meaning, I had to resolve the problem of my graduate school novel. How could I shape a pattern of meaning and still allow characters freedom? The two needs seemed to conflict.

The possibility of writing fiction opened to me when I finally understood that patterns of meaning are not shaped by the conscious intent of the writer; they emerge naturally from the freely chosen actions of the characters. Aristotle's discussion was more than technical. A beginning followed by a middle and a discernible end is more than a sequence. It is a purposeful action, an image of the Christian affirmation of a linear, purposeful history ordered by a creative God. The story itself is its meaning. A writer's task is first to tell it and second to trust it.

As I reflected on this deceptively simple solution to what I had thought was a conundrum, I realized my difficulties with fiction stemmed from a totally different problem. My interest, when I thought I was doing fiction, had been autobiography. Without knowing it, I had been trying to impose the orderliness of a beginning, middle and end onto the wild unruliness of my life. I had been trying to trim the loose ends of my experience to find a core of meaning, and in doing that I had failed to grasp how radical the imaginative act is that allows one to leap from life to fiction. To write fiction I had to sacrifice that drive for self-knowledge appropriate to me as a poet and seek instead to know, to love and to honor my characters and the world in which they lived.

Finally understanding that, when I began to write the stories that became *Nightwatch* I used fragments of autobiography to construct my story. But I did not write autobiographically. Neither Mark nor Dickie, the two main characters of my story, is me. Neither is the mother or the father of the story my mother or father. Mark and Dickie do things I never did. Mark witnesses a couple copulating in the woods. His actions lead to Dickie's falling while caving and shattering a leg. Mark is insensitive to Dickie after the injury, and, finally, he is deliberately cruel to his father. I am guilty of none of those things.

Mark and Dickie also do things I have done. Early in the story Mark smashes a toy rifle against a tree. I once did that, but I've forgotten why. Mark tricks Dickie into swimming a freezing mountain stream. In my teens I did that to a friend. Later Mark runs cross-country. I did that also, but I was, at my best, the seventh man on a seven-man team. None of these examples amounts to more than a curiosity. Each is merely an external correspondence, a coincidence.

Sometimes, however, what begins as a simple autobiographical correspondence is transformed by the imagination. An example of this transformation of autobiography into fiction occurs near the end of *Nightwatch*. Mark, in love with Mary and suffering the usual adolescent traumas of desire and guilt, is working as a night watchman at a church camp. During his rounds one evening, he sits watching over a meadow and sees in it the figure of a strange shambling man, a tramp who threatens him with a gun before fleeing into the night. The next evening, at a cabin away from camp on his day off, he dreams:

> He was sitting under the tree overlooking the meadow. Halfway down it a hunched figure rose from a depression. Behind it the red glow of a fire appeared. Faint music drifted towards him. Other shadowy shapes, circling the fire, joined the first. Somehow he knew he knew them, so he rose and went forward. As he moved through the field, he felt himself grow small until he was a mere nub of fear. Then the hunched figure, an old man with a long gray beard, stepped from the circle. He took his hand, drew him from the world, and led him to a willowy and laughing girl. He joined their hands, stepped aside, and took up a fiddle. The circle closed, and he began calling a square dance. Mark gave himself to it. Whirling with the girl on his arm, he became part of the pattern, a community in consort, united in joy. And then he saw the girl was Mary.

> Suddenly the music ended. The dance dissolved. The dancers scattered. Mary held his hand and led him through the woods. Huge footsteps pounded behind them. Though they pushed through the grassblades and scrambled over sticks and stones, they were too slow. Mary fell, cowering. "Get up! Run!" Mark pleaded. He turned. Though he died, whatever followed would not harm her. A human hand reached down and lifted him into the air. He fought and wriggled as it drew him close to a pasty, empty face. Then he screamed. The face was his own.

Here, near the climax of the novel, I have given Mark something internal from my character, a dream I actually had. Though I have almost transcribed my dream into Mark's experience, Mark's dream is not my dream. In the real world of my life, my dream was the dream of a middle-aged man subconsciously acknowledging his deep complicity in humankind's rapacious devouring of nature. In the fictive world of my novel it becomes by an act of imagination the dream of a young man encountering for the first time his violent, self-destructive other. Where my dream is just another dream, Mark's dream, occurring within the unfolding of his story, becomes a transforming experience, the starting point of his salvation.

What is crucial to understand about the imaginative act is that it begins with an event, the meaning of which is, though partially understood, ultimately unknowable. It is partially understood, as I described understanding my dream above, because humans are gifted with the ability to make connections and to verbalize them. Mature adults, however, recognize that every event is also unknowable in any definitive sense, for it has occurred within the unfolding of an unfinished, unbounded life.

The writer of fiction accepts this tension in human existence and gives events knowable fictive meaning by placing them in the limited context of a self-contained, invented world. In other words, the fiction writer engages in a deliberate, conscious simplification, a reduction of the unknowable complexities of the actual world to the knowable clarity of a completed action. In creating this completeness, which by its very nature is an affirmation of purposeful action, the writer makes a fictive world stand as an image of that completeness and wholeness Christians ascribe by faith to history. This is true whether the author gives consent to such an affirmation or not. The form itself is Christian. This does not mean that fiction is simple or simplistic. It remains complex and, since it must be read in the world, mysterious; but within its telling it is not, like life, unknowable.

I remember two things now as I begin a story. First, the story itself is point enough. I needn't worry about its meaning. And second, I cannot seek to know myself by writing tales. Whatever meaning might develop as a tale is told is meaning for that tale only. The events of my life are larger—to be understood only in the larger tale the Creator is working in history. For now we see through a glass darkly. For now I make images that tell my faith in the wholeness and goodness of that larger tale I live in.

Truth by Moonlight

When I was an undergraduate at Houghton College in the mid-1960s, the literature curriculum focused on genre. Four were taught: poetry, fiction, drama and prose. Each student chose three to study. Prose was taught by a legendary figure, a thin, aging but formidable woman called Doc Jo who had been at Houghton since the 1920s. Doc Jo believed in structure and formal study. I believed in spontaneity and in picking up knowledge like burrs. Fear kept me out of her class. But even if I hadn't feared the work, I would have stayed out of her class because I had no interest in prose. Accepting a definition of prose as nonfiction, I had no idea how open to mystery it was. I thought in simple terms and assumed prose writers told the truth and nothing but the truth. I thought they dealt in answers. Though I wasn't ready to accept answers, I think I needed to believe they were there to be had when and if I ever wanted them. Discovering it otherwise might have shaken my uneasy faith in a meaning-filled world.

My study of prose began only when I began to establish myself as a poet. A few teachers in evangelical colleges and a few church leaders who knew my work invited me to visit their schools or churches to talk about Christianity and the arts. A coward, or a wise fool, I decided I needed a text before me to safely address what I knew would be a cautiously skeptical audience. I began to write essays, tentative explorations of what I thought my poems were about. When they were written, I spoke them out loud. I testified to my experience.

Those first few essays determined the nature of my prose. It was personal; I relied on telling my story to make my points. It was informal and oral; I chose a language held in common with my audience, and I consciously used the rhythms of spoken sentences to hold my thoughts.

And it was tentative; I set forth what I was thinking at the time, not a final word on any subject.

Though my style has perhaps over the years grown a bit more complex, I think it has not changed much. I still like to grow plain statements out of personal stories. My voice remains simple and direct, closely connected to speech. But as the years have passed, my tentativeness has grown, and I find prose harder and harder to write. I am less and less sure of what I have to say. This uncertainty has nothing to do with any lack of faith or conviction. It has rather to do with three shifts in my thinking. First, I have an increasing respect for the wondrous mystery of my life. Second, I am more aware of the limitations of language. And third, I am dumbfounded by my finiteness before the infiniteness of truth.

ONE

Sometimes when I sit before a blank sheet of paper I feel trapped in my own experience. The personal definition of my testimony isolates me, and I see myself as nothing more than an egocentric scribbler, playing words like a trickster, calling attention to myself to escape my loneliness, pretending to believe someone out there hears and cares. At those times I wonder what right I have to speak.

Early in the opening chapter of *Walden*, Thoreau composed an apology for writing in the first person. He wrote, "I should not talk so much about myself if there were anybody else whom I knew as well. Unfortunately, I am confined to this theme by the narrowness of my experience." A century later, in the preface to his collected essays, E. B. White blithely accepted the congenital self-centeredness of the personal essayist and made a virtue of what is commonly thought to be a flaw. Neither writer's defense seems sufficient to me, for neither writer engages the tension I feel between my writer's need to focus on my own experience and my Christian responsibility to refuse the trap of self-absorption and to reach out to identify with the experience of others. The issue for me is this: Can I have it both ways?

I think I can. Part of the good news of the gospel is I am not alone; I am part of the body of Christ. When I speak, I speak as a member of the body of Christ to others who are or who potentially are also members of that body. Just as what happens to my eye is of consequence to my hand, so what happens to me is of consequence to my reader. My words on the page work as a message from the eye to the hand: "Reach out. Touch what is beautiful. Draw back. Danger is ahead." Understood this way, my speaking personally becomes not indulgence but the necessary communication of one part of the body with another. My reader and I need each other. In the sharing of the personal we grow. One's experience enlarges the experience of the body. Still it is sometimes hard to understand how this happens.

I remember a spring afternoon more than fifteen years ago. I had spent the morning in the garden setting out cauliflower and sowing the seeds of winter squash along the fence. As always after garden tending, the quiet pleasure of having done good work filled me. I was at peace, comfortable in body and soul. In that state I went to my study to work on an essay I called "Craft and Holiness." Before I had written a paragraph something in me woke and destroyed my peaceable kingdom.

Outside my open door my wife was combing my young daughter's hair, which heat and humidity had snarled. My wife pulled and tugged. My daughter wiggled, complained, jerked away and, finally, burst into tears.

Totally incapable of comprehending the universal motherly need to banish tangles from the earth, I thought, "I'm writing about holiness. Must you make such devilish noise?" Stupidly, I opened my mouth, expressed my thought and turned mere noise into strife. I wonder, still, what right I have to speak of holiness.

Shortly after that hair-combing incident, I was involved in interviewing a candidate for a faculty position at the college where I teach. During the interview, a certain amount of jesting resulting from the candidate's earnest remarks about integrating faith and learning prompted one of my colleagues to say, "We live in the ironic mode here." The accuracy of his quip caught me by surprise, and I have remembered it, not because it describes the atmosphere where I work but because it describes the nature of my life; it captures the disparity between my aspirations and my behavior and focuses it through the lens of comedy. It is through that lens I see my way to write.

If I were to choose any words from Scripture to characterize my experience, I would choose Saint Paul's: "For the good that I would I do not: but the evil which I would not, that I do" (Romans 7:19). Though some suggest that these words of Paul describe his pre-Christian condition, my Presbyterian education tells me that interpretation is wishful. Though I know Paul has seen the seventh heaven, I am convinced he describes the falling short he daily experiences. I know he describes the falling short I experience, and I am sobered and chagrined.

If this failing were the total of our lives, neither Paul nor I would have much hope. There is, however, another part to the comedy. The script calls for a conclusion we can only dimly understand. We are not destined for failure. We will by grace be made perfect—revealed to be an adopted child of the One who tells the story we live.

With each passing day, as I stumble bewildered through the twisting narrative of dailiness, my life grows more complicated, unmanageable and incomprehensible. Friends suffer diseases. Parents age and grow weak. Children endure oppression. Relationships break. I despair of ever understanding how God is present in this world, and I cannot speak the truth. When I am overwhelmed by this despair, when I yield to the feeling that I am not good enough to speak of holiness or any other theme, I return to my understanding of this comic mystery, my sense of my life as an action rising toward restoration, as a source of hope. Though my understanding is partial, it is enough. I live in hope not knowledge. Trusting the promise that I will someday know as I am known, I am content to fall down, to speak my personal words and do the best I can.

TWO

I do the best I can in a language determined by my life within the Christian community. I grew up reading and memorizing the King James Bible. I think in its rhythms, and I think in its images. Beyond that and, perhaps more important, because of the primacy given Scripture in my youth, I continue to give a primacy to the word in my thinking. I cannot be converted to the visually oriented emphasis of the media-driven culture I'm doomed to live in. I believe in discourse, and I believe that discourse is built on a traditional way of speaking about the world.

A friend who professes no faith I know of once said to me, "I envy you your Christian images. They give you a way of saying things I only feel." Recently I read John Gardner's *On Becoming a Novelist* with a senior seminar in writing. We spent an hour on one sentence: "Once one has made a strong psychological investment in a certain kind of language, one has trouble understanding that it distorts reality." When I asked the class to consider the implications of the sentence for the evangelical writer, they immediately fastened on the peculiar physical squeamishness of evangelical readers and directed their remarks to issues of freedom and censorship. While they may be right—a refusal to use a word may be a fault—I think they missed the point.

Language and reality are inextricably bound, so bound that some critics argue that reality is linguistic. I think common sense refutes them; the world is larger and more complex than my linguistic structure. But common sense also grants some truth to their position; my expressible knowledge of that world is limited by my language—not limited by my facility with language but by language itself. Just as I have no direct apprehension of God, I have no direct apprehension of the world. Language mediates the world to me. The world I know and speak is made of words.

Given this, I can imagine three strategies for how I use my words. One, I can choose silence, refuse to speak and try to apprehend the world (and God) in wordless perfection. This is the way of the mystic and of my late dog Poon, a blue tick hound, who while he lived never spoke a word but seemed to know all things. Two, I can choose to accept the language and the givens of my culture group as final, be molded by them into the likeness of every other member of the group, and speak clichés and platitudes. This is the choice I think Gardner was cautioning against in his sentence. It is also the choice most people make. Third, I can consciously choose the creative responsibility of language. Consider the creation narrative in Genesis. For six days God labored speaking the world into being. He did not labor as an engineer. He labored as a poet. Then he rested or, as a wise man pointed out, he created rest. After resting, he assigned Adam the task of naming the creation. By assigning him this task, God involved him in the completion of the creation; he involved him in it in such a manner that he could know nothing apart from his linguistic involvement with it, his relation to it. Adam's reality is relational, discovered new every day, evolving. It is never complete, for it exists in the interaction of the physical world and language. It is intentionally open. This does not, however, mean that my language has no connection with what has been said before. My language is traditional. It is alive—rooted and growing.

This openness, this simultaneous rootedness and changeableness, is the genius of prose. Of all the genres it most clearly revels in the inexpressible wonder of the continuing creation of the world.

THREE

The community I grew up in not only shaped my understanding of language, it shaped my understanding of God. It taught me to be chummy with the deity, that *he* is my friend and buddy. It taught me to speak of *him* as *Father.* Though I italicize *Father* and the masculine pronouns as I reflect on this heritage, I have no intention to renounce it. I often think of God as *Father,* and I find it helpful. I use the italics to indicate that *Father* does not define the limits of how I think of God.

If I am to write, I must use words and images available to me and to my audience. Even God in choosing language and incarnation—word and flesh—as vehicles for revelation accepted the limits I cannot transcend. So I say *Father.* I say *Father* for two reasons. One, the image of God as *Father* is common to Scripture. Two, the image of God as *Father* speaks to me. I was blessed to have a father who loved me and made—not often in words—his love known.

But I say *Father* recognizing there are those not blessed as I am. I have sat with students and heard stories of abuse, of fathers sexually using their daughters, of fathers imposing fantasies of success on their sons, and I know the image of God as *Daddy,* God as *Abba Father,* is a shattered image in this shattered world. Nevertheless my bondage to images remains. And shattered though it is, the image of *Father* remains potentially meaningful, for we all know what a father ought to be. *Father* as an image is unavailable to us only when we cease to understand its frailty. When out of desperation or weakness we reduce the infinite to fit the stretch of our imagination, we commit idolatry.

One winter night, not long ago, I went out to empty the kitchen compost in the barrel near the back of the garden. I wore no jacket since I did not intend to be outside long. The moon shone down on the snow-covered lawn, and I walked in a cold light that was almost tactile. I emptied the compost and turned back to the house, but I did not go in. I stood instead, the cold soaking into me, and looked up at the moon. It was as white as the snow at my feet. Though there was no wind where I stood, sheer pellucid clouds raced in front of it. Shadows of craters pocked its sullen face, and I stared—spellbound, moonstruck, whatever it is one feels gazing at that haunting disk in the night. I thought of the men who have walked there and how little that knowledge has changed my imagination. The moon remains the moon, and I thought about its light.

Moonlight is sunlight reflected, sunlight made bearable to our fragile vision. Moonlight is an image, a way of seeing the sun. I stood there, the clouds passing by. The craters outlined a familiar face—the man in the moon. Though I shivered, I was comfortable. I felt chummy with that old guy.

I've never looked straight at the sun. I never plan to. I'm content with moonlight. But be sure, I don't confuse it with the burning reality behind it.

FOUR

The peculiar difficulty I face as a prose writer comes clear to me when I think of that curious encounter between Jesus and Pilate recorded in each of the Gospels. If I line up the accounts and consider them together, I see very quickly that they differ. Though sharing a common inspiration, each writer tells the story from his own limited perspective and intention. No one writer is either right or wrong in his telling. Neither is some composite of the four accounts the whole story. The whole truth is not given to us. There is something beyond the reach of the text, something puzzling that surfaces in each telling and surfaces most bewilderingly in John's account.

Pilate has asked Jesus if he is a king. Jesus answers, "Thou sayest that I am a king. To this end was I born, and for this cause came I into the world, that I should bear witness unto the truth. Every one that is of the truth heareth my voice" (John 18:37). Then Pilate asks Jesus, "What is truth?" John does not record any answer Jesus gives. He tells us instead that Pilate turns away and goes out to the waiting Jews, who call for the release of Barabbas.

Drawing conclusions based on the silence of Jesus and Pilate's marveling at it in the other Gospels, I assume Jesus simply stands before Pilate without speaking.

But why? Why is Jesus silent?

His refusal to speak at such a moment must be more than a rhetorical ploy. Surely he is not deliberately angering Pilate, forcing the judgment that means his condemnation and our salvation. I think Jesus is silent because he is the Christ, because he stands before Pilate the embodiment of truth, the Word made flesh. No word uttered in a human tongue could contain the reality of his presence.

He did not need words to speak truth. I do.

That is my burden, my joy and my hope.

Part Four

In the Care of the Spirit

In the Care of the Spirit

ONE

I'm sitting in my office at Houghton College looking across the quad to the chapel. Though a few patches of snow remain, the green of spring is rising like light from the ground. Before me I have an extensive form to fill out; if I succeed in answering all the questions correctly, I may be invited to appear on a big-time Christian television show. I'm pondering two questions in particular: "Date born again?" and "When did Jesus Christ become more than just a name to you?"

They are not easy questions for me. Jesus is more than a name; he is the incarnate Son in whom I live and move and have my being. I have no doubt I am born again. Yet I have difficulty with the question, for my Christian experience refuses to lie down in orderly phrases.

I ought to be able to do something about that; I am, after all, a writer. But a writer does not subdue experience with verbs and nouns. A writer, like everyone else, is as mute before the mystery of God's presence as a turtle. Nevertheless I am called to try.

Perhaps my first conscious act of worship occurred when I was eight or nine. I got up from my bed on Christmas Eve, not to see if Santa Claus had come but to write a poem about the Christ Child. My mother still has this poem in a scrapbook, and as I remember it, I am tempted to believe it marks my beginning and my first concern as a writer—the meaning of the incarnation.

But I suspect that is reading backwards into experience (inventing a coherence). From that point, at least, Christ has been more than a name. Was I at that point born again? I don't know. I'm sure I was in the care of the Spirit.

A few years later (I could date this), I attended a summer camp run by the First Presbyterian Church of Pittsburgh. There one afternoon I sat at the edge of a hemlock grove, read my Bible and prayed a conventional prayer for Jesus to be in my life. I meant it as maturely as I knew how. Was I at that point born again? I think so. But I'm not sure the words I said had much to do with it, and nothing I could see in my life changed. I told no one about my prayer—this in fact may be the first recounting of it. Nothing in my life changed, because I was pointed by my family and by my church in the direction of Christ. My prayer was not a turnabout; it was simply an assent, an acknowledgment of what was already taking place.

These two experiences seem to me to be characteristic of my spiritual life. I choose to worship. I give assent to the Spirit dwelling in me, leading me, calling me forward to a fellowship I can't refuse. What that fellowship includes is what I explore, what I write about.

TWO

My father introduced me to the adult world when I was twelve; he took me on a fishing and camping trip with his friends. The first night in camp, Pete Harris, who would later loan me a shotgun and sell me a "worn-out" pair of Converse waders I'd use for fifteen years, began my initiation. I was sitting listening to talk when Pete came up out of the dark from the river carrying a stringer of catfish.

"Here; hold these," he said to me. Then he began rummaging in a plywood box of utensils under the table in the lean-to. Producing a pair of pliers, a claw hammer and a spike, he picked up a lantern and motioned for me to follow him. I did. Stopping beside a stump about twenty yards from camp, he asked, "You know how to skin the cat?"

I knew he wasn't referring to the child's jungle gym trick, so I said, "No."

"Watch" was all he answered.

He took the first catfish off the stringer, placed it on the stump and drove a nail through its head. Its tail thunked once as the spike went in. "Nerves," Pete said. Then he took out his pocketknife, licked the hair on his arm and shaved a spot clean. "You'll sooner cut yourself with a dull knife than a sharp one," he instructed me as he made a quick incision behind the catfish's head and loosened the skin. "Now here's the trick to skinning the cat," he said. He picked up the pliers, grasped the skin and peeled it back as if he were removing a sock. The clean white of the flesh shown like a slice of moon on the dark stump. I stood in awe. One motion of the knife severed the head, and the cat was cleaned.

"Your turn," he said. And I set eagerly to work. For the next four years, until my brother at last turned twelve, I cleaned every fish in that camp and learned my place in my father's world.

THREE

Some years ago I attended a gathering of writers at the Library of Congress to discuss the state of creative writing in the nation's colleges and universities. The first session started slowly; for nearly an hour a panel of distinguished writers argued over whether the adjective *creative* should ever modify the noun *writing*. Finally, as if he were uttering the last word on the subject, one said, "Have you ever heard of noncreative writing?" Everyone laughed, and the panel at last moved on to another subject.

Sitting in my study tonight, I'm uneasy with the glibness of the laughter in Washington, and I'm uneasy with the quick dismissal of the question.

I have heard of noncreative writing. I read it every day. I read it in student papers. I read it in interoffice memos. I read it in the newspapers. And I read it in the work of "important" writers. Noncreative writing is destructive writing, writing that destroys either the potential of language to express the nuances of meaning or the potential of human beings to experience their place—a little lower than the angels—in creation.

Creative writing is writing that seeks to discover and articulate these potentials. There is surprisingly little of it, for it is difficult, and often writers, mistaking platitude for vision, settle for restating what others have already said. Readers seem to like that, and many writers have become wealthy pandering to them. But creative writing is risky writing. It is living by faith. It is stepping into the dark without a light.

In one of his rare essays Robert Frost wrote, "Every time a poem is written, every time a short story is written, it is written not by cunning, but by belief." Frost, I realize, is talking about a belief in the thing being made, but his remark suggests a Christian parallel that extends beyond the limits of creative writing. Just as creative writers live by hope, looking ahead to the work that must be unknown until it is discovered in the act of writing, Christians live by hope, looking ahead to the new creation, discovering in the act of living the whole persons they are becoming as Christ works his transformation in them.

FOUR

Though I have always been eager to learn, I have never been a good student. Looking back, I suspect I drove more than one teacher to despair. But I am thinking as a teacher, considering how I'd like to be heard, casting the best light I can on my profession. All students are difficult. And well they should be. It is their persons that are being fashioned, and I believe they are justified in every defense they fashion against our manipulation.

I started to play defense in sixth grade when I encountered the first of many teachers who would have my best interest at heart. Like Thoreau, who wrote, "If I knew for a certainty that a man was coming to my house with the conscious design of doing me good, I should run for my life," I preferred to commit my own sins and discover my own virtues. Most of all I preferred to choose my own character.

I entered high school with one passion: I had grown up in the country and I loved the outdoors. From the earliest moment I could escape my mother's eye, I took to the woods. I wasn't a naturalist; my responses were intuitive and relational. I loved what I saw without naming it or desiring to control it. That state, of course, could not last; love without naming, without knowledge, cannot be responsibly sustained. Though I could not have said that then, I think I knew it, and I eagerly enrolled in William J. Barker's biology class.

A man of gargantuan girth threatening the seams of his striped, dark blue three-piece suit, William J. Barker was a legend in the school. It was said that he had once lifted an inattentive football player from his seat, heaved him through the door and continued his lecture without missing a word. No one could confirm the story. When asked about it William J. just smiled. His academic specialty was a rare breed of bog turtle found only in eastern Pennsylvania, and the high point of the class was a turtle hunt each spring. William J., safari-jacketed and knee-deep in a Pennsylvania bog, was as impressive and rare as a feeding moose.

Early on William J. and I got on well. Though he told me my drawing of a paramecium looked more like the sole of his shoe after he had walked through cut wet grass than any single-celled organism he'd ever seen, he recognized I had an interest and saw in me potential. He invited me to be his "gofer" and work with him outside of class. I readily agreed, but I soon learned that being a disciple of William J. could be a problem, for in his mind a student with potential was a student to be guided and shaped—shaped into an image of himself. I didn't have the girth for it, and before long I disappointed him. Disappointed, William J. was dangerous. For my own good, to keep me from failing to be all he would have me be, he began to apply the screws. He graded me harder than he had when he favored me. He belittled me in front of the class to spur me on. He assigned me detention for trumped-up offenses.

I have no question that William J. was a good man, no question that his intention for me was good. But William J. could not separate his own desires for me from my desires for me. Far from being able to walk in another's shoes, he could not resist, could not even recognize, his own need to walk over another's will to impose his own. For all his gifts, William J. failed as a teacher. He was so taken with his own power he could not see the footsteps he left behind were on student backs. By the end of the year I hated William J. and had given my allegiance to writing.

Along with that allegiance I discovered what would be my second concern as a writer—understanding and articulating my place in the physical world. With time and coupled with my understanding of incarnation, this would grow into an inclusive ecological vision alternately informed by and informing my faith.

FIVE

As spring approaches, I've been going to the woodlot each Saturday to observe the winter's decline and to learn the changes being worked in the life there. Last week the little creek in the gully was partially thawed. Fine lace decorated the open falls, filigree patterns spread across the frozen pools, and the music of running water played against the screech of a blue jay. This week, however, cold locked the music in silence, and I walked up the stream, my steps obliterating the sharp prints of the deer moving to the open field below the woodlot.

Where the stream forks, I turned up the hill, zigged and zagged around several large hemlock stumps, and headed toward the old orchard now grown up in thornapple. I stopped beside a groundhog hole and looked back. A spike tail, fourteen or fifteen inches long, protruded from behind the nearest stump. Carelessly I shifted into a comfortable position and waited. At my movement the tail disappeared. A moment later, a pink, snubbed nose emerged. A creamy white face with black, deep-set eyes and delicate black ears followed. And then the thick body, creamy white but overlaid with silver gray hairs that shimmered when he ruffled his fur against the wind.

My first impulse was to rush forward, cover the fifteen feet between us to see if he would play possum. But I remained still.

He looked at me, shrugged his silver shoulders, turned and, lifting each pink-soled foot high above the snow as if shaking the cold from it before choosing to touch it down again, stepped lightly away. His naked tail, never bending or touching the ground, stayed spiked.

Making no effort to either hide or close the gap between us, I followed him through the orchard. When he stopped to snuffle among the leaves in the thawed rings around the trees, I stopped. When he moved on, I moved on. At the stock fence marking the line between my woodlot and the college farm, he paused, placed his front paws on a wire and deftly lifted himself through one of the squares a foot from the ground. I leaned on a fence post and watched him stroll into the open pasture, his amazing tail still rigid an inch above the ground.

Since I wasn't going to follow, I clapped my hands and shouted, sending up a kind of praise from the fenceline. A chestnut gelding across the field snorted and made a short run toward me, but the opossum, oblivious or accepting the applause as his due, padded on. He flexed his shoulders in the wind, sending a wave of silver down his back, and ambled toward a lone apple tree that I expected him to climb. He paused beneath it, looked up and then, content with whatever knowledge he had, suddenly dropped out of sight into a hole.

SIX

In the mail today I received a copy of a review of my new book of poems, *Country Labors*. A brief quote from it gives its flavor:

> Our "narrow-mindedness" keeps us from recommending it because of what would be considered favorable references to smoking and drinking—and, even

more, to its use of profanity. Most are brief, . . . and few have any semblance of spiritual content.

Some years ago I would have feigned arrogance to help me cope with such pernicious literalism. I would have slandered the reviewer privately and vented steam from my ears. (Some years ago? I haven't gotten that far toward sainthood.) But I've learned that that response only widens the chasm I seek to leap. I share membership in the body of Christ with that reviewer. Rather than be angry, I must remember that the community I have chosen for my primary audience—the local community I dwell in and the larger evangelical Christian community it is part of—includes a large portion of similar readers, and that it is my task to make my experience available to them. More than that, my relationship to this community or audience is the third (and perhaps most troubling) of my three central themes.

Edward Abbey, one of my favorite "pagan" writers, wrote, "The writer speaks not *to* his audience (who wants to listen to lectures?) but *for* them, expressing their thoughts and emotions through the imaginative power of his art." I've come to accept Abbey's statement as a true expression of my relationship to my audience. I read that way. I seek out writers who through their vision make contact with my experience and vision. This is not limiting or narrowing. It is rather expansive, inclusive, an opening up to the world. I try to write the same way, to speak for that community I would not—could not if I would—escape membership in.

But in a profound sense my relationship to my chosen community and audience is conditional. They have not fully chosen me, for I bring to my membership a personal history of an existence in a larger, less exclusive community—a membership I have not rejected, a membership I will not reject.

SEVEN

Among the first mature poems I would write was a series of poems about my father's family. I recognized in the extended family, all living together in one small valley and hillside, a core of relationships which would serve as a foundation for any sense of community I could ever have. Within that family I did not choose were men and women—both good and bad—to whom I owed my life and character. And at the center of that family was my grandfather.

I began to write:

> Spilled from a mildewed box
> you are
> the pieces of a faded puzzle
> working alone   I have spread your dull colors
> face up on the table
> but have done no more
> you are
> difficult
> I have tried all the combinations
> but failed   to build even your border
> for you have given me extra pieces
> and withheld the one I need

As I read those words now, I realize how much they began; I realize how much they are about.

My grandfather was not an easy man. Though I wrote about him as an adult, I wrote from a child's memory. Though I wrote from love, I offended my aunts, and my grandmother gave no clear indication of her feelings other than to grin and say to me, "You're a sly one, writing about your grandfather." I wish I'd asked what she meant.

But that doesn't matter now.

My grandfather was a sly one himself. An incident that occurred when I was about five comes back to me. I was playing near the chicken house. He was drinking a beer, sitting on a stone step between the lane and the long walk to the house. Somehow I annoyed a banty rooster, and it turned its wing-flapping fury on me. Overwhelmed, I fled. And the rooster followed, stabbing its beak time after time into the tenderness of my backside. My grandfather never moved. The louder I screamed, the harder he laughed.

When my mother appeared to rescue me and turned her righteous anger toward him, he rocked with joy. A few days later, he sat me down at his table, and while he laughed, I gnawed in innocent satisfaction the drumsticks that had chased me home.

But that doesn't matter now either.

I read my words and wonder who it is I address. My family? Myself? God? Why do I need to speak as I do? And what is the puzzle I want to complete? Dare I venture an answer?

If not an answer, a method. All my life I've spent picking up little pieces of experience, turning them about in my imagination, fitting them into the larger picture I've never seen—it was against the rules in my grandfather's house to do a puzzle with the picture before you. We had to work blind.

And that is how I write. Blindly, I examine relationships, fit pieces together, try combinations until I find sense and coherence. But unlike the pieces of the puzzles on my grandfather's table that were eventually all accounted for when he produced the secreted last one from his pocket, the pieces of the puzzle I ponder multiply. Every space I clear, fitting a piece into place, is filled with a new one.

EIGHT

Everyone called him "the Kraut." It seemed right in those days when skins were thick and ethnic nicknames stuck. He was German and his lifeblood was beer. His real name was Will. He was the warehouseman and truck driver at Smith-High Corporation, the small construction company where I had worked summers since I was fifteen. Now I was twenty-one, a college dropout—working a dead-end job, enjoying mindless labor, thinking about getting my life together.

A day didn't go by that Will didn't give me free advice: "Go back to school, Jackie-boy. You don't want to be doing this at fifty." I knew what he meant. Unloading a tractor-trailer load of hollow metal doors with the summer sun beating down gave meaning to the word *work*. But I wasn't in a hurry. The draft had passed me by—my one good eye wasn't enough for them—and the prospect of Vietnam that was troubling my generation had faded from my consciousness. I was young and strong, and Will had taught me well. "Never use your back when you can use your brain," he'd said until I'd made it habit.

We worked easily together, companionably, sharing a rhythm of labor that comes of long collaboration and understanding. Over the years Will had told me his life story: his childhood in an orphanage, his teenaged visit to a cathouse, the best years of his life as a serviceman in Germany after the war, his marriage, the increasing trials of his marriage and his whining, self-centered, acquisitive kids. Most of this story he'd revealed sitting in the cool dark of some hidden workingmen's bar in a rundown section of town. We'd be out on a delivery and he'd develop a thirst. He'd slip the truck down some alley and park it out of sight, and we'd enter the back door. Usually he'd call in his number, and then we'd sit. He'd nurse an Iron City, and I'd put away a thick buttermilk. They were good times. But they were off the record.

Smith-High Corporation was owned by my uncle, and I understood the importance of silence. Several years before, Will had had an accident with the company truck. Two people had been killed, and though he hadn't had a beer that day, my uncle was sensitive to his drinking. My presence with the Kraut meant I was trusted by two people.

One hot day, returning from a delivery, we stopped, parking the truck as always behind the bar. We entered the welcoming stillness, ordered our usuals and sat. Halfway through his beer, Will started to talk. "My wife wants to move to California," he said. "She's got a brother there hauls garbage for the city. She says I can drive for him." He lifted his glass and drank. "Sheet, Jackie, I don't want to be no goddamned garbageman."

I drank my buttermilk. He motioned for a second beer. "She's going, Jackie. She says I can come if I want." Then he fell silent. We sat a long time and were late getting back.

When I swung down from the cab to block the traffic so Will could back into the warehouse, my uncle met me in the street.

"Did Will stop for beer?" he snapped.

I looked away from him. Will's round, red face filled the mirror, but I didn't see him there. I saw him slumped on that barstool, repeating over and over, "A garbageman. A god-damned garbageman. That's all she thinks of me."

"Don't look away," my uncle barked. "Answer." I opened my mouth but found no words.

"Never mind," my uncle said. "You don't have to say anything." In that moment I think he realized what he was asking and knew it wasn't fair. I think sadness broke his anger.

He turned and fired the Kraut.

Will pulled the truck onto the sidewalk and followed my uncle to his office. A few minutes later he came out. Nearly in tears he put his hand on my shoulder and said, "Jackie-boy, it wasn't your fault." Will shook his head, then walked away.

I watched him go—out the door, down the sidewalk and around the corner. When he was gone, I climbed into the cab and backed the truck into the warehouse.

NINE

From this dark wood, dormant
in star shine,
the squirrels still in the bounty
of oak abundance,
the mice curled close beneath
the insulating snow,
nothing is far.

Here above the valley,
in body numbing cold I wait
open to what descends.
Nothing breaks over me. Night is all.
It holds me,
and lost in the loss
of sense, I ask nothing.

From the houses below
where friends dwell in peace
lights as steady as stars
rise to greet my watch.
No angel will descend.
All there is to see I see;
Christ is in His world.

TEN

When I arrived, a somewhat disgruntled transfer student, at Houghton College for the spring semester in 1965, I had no intentions of taking a writing course. The following fall, however, to buy time and to be with friends who were writing majors, I enrolled in Writers' Workshop and came under the tutelage of Al Campbell. At first I wasn't impressed. In fact, if I'm even half truthful, I have to admit I was arrogant and scornful. The man didn't seem to know anything. No matter what we wrote, he had something good to say. I sat in his class, and I thought he was the oldest young man I'd ever met.

No one incident changed my mind, but I remember one clearly. After reading Karl Shapiro, I wrote a set of poems in prose. Shapiro had written, "Why should a grown man speak in rhyme?" Fully expecting to antagonize Professor Campbell, I turned in my poems. His response stunned me. "These are interesting," he said. "What do you suppose it is that makes a poem a poem?" Then the class talked for an hour. He had taken my experiment more seriously than I had.

About then I began to understand. Al Campbell wasn't the least bit interested in teaching me to write. His only concern was that I *learn* to write what I wanted to write. He was giving me freedom, and if I wanted to write poems in prose that was fine with him. He never imagined, and I never told him, that I had written those poems only to aggravate. I was the one who knew nothing. He was the teacher I had wanted, and I was too pig-headed to know it.

When I think of him now, I think of him as "the Great Encourager." His gift as a teacher was not the gift of criticism. It was rather the gift of generous admiration. He saw what we might become and praised that. He valued us before we valued ourselves. Like the Christ he served, he loved us, and his love gave us value.

In 1968 I joined the Houghton faculty. Ten of us shared an office in Fancher Hall. I shared a desk with Al, but since there was only one chair, we never sat at it together. Still, I came to know him as I could not when I was in his class, and without his knowing it (without my knowing it) I became again his student. It happened this way. I had thought, along with my classmates, that Al was about fifty. What I learned when I returned was that Al was sixty-six and facing forced retirement. I was to be his replacement. Then I learned from Al the story of his life. The years of rough work. The late return to high school. Then college and marriage. The years at Moody. And at last his tenure at Houghton.

As he gradually told his story (I did not get it all at one sitting), I began to appreciate the quality of mind that drove him. I can characterize his discriminating openness and committed liveliness by no other word than *passion*. He was unhindered by fear and totally oblivious to what "correct minds" might think. He was, in short, free. And he gave his freedom to us.

After Al retired I did not see him as often as I would have liked, and too often when I did it was when I visited him in the hospital. That's where I saw him last, the day the Buffalo Bills, on their way to a Super Bowl appearance, destroyed the Raiders. We watched the game half-heartedly and visited. I don't remember much of what we said, but the day was a gift, for as I was about to leave, his wife, Marge, asked me to pray with them. My last words with Al were addressed to the Lord, and they were words of thanks. One thing I might have said but didn't was this: "Al, you're the youngest old man I've ever met."

ELEVEN

Three of us lined the church pew waiting for Communion to be served. My wife, Linda, my daughter, Melissa, and myself.

Melissa was about five, at that unpredictable age when parents never know what might happen next. We were sitting too far forward for my comfort, and as the elements passed up and down the pews, I was paying more attention to Melissa, who was drawing, than I was to repentant thoughts or the words being spoken from the table. Suddenly, watching her, I realized something was happening in me. That afternoon I wrote,

> The blandness of his body
> still in my mouth,
> his blood
> cupped in my hands,
> I pause for prayer.
>
> Beside me my daughter
> draws a man
> with a heart-shaped head.
>
> She tells me it is me.
> The sureness of this hour
> is reconciliation.
> The bread, the blood, her love
> confound my double nature.

Melissa's drawing and whispered phrase, "This is you," were an illumination. The exchange between us was an exchange in grace—Christ dwelling in her greeting, Christ dwelling in me. I was stunned.

The exchange, however, did not end there; the whole congregation participated. Christ went out from each worshiper to greet Christ in each worshiper. The church was filled with Christ. In that moment I knew the mystical body was incarnate.

In the years since then I've been acutely aware that I am never alone, that I am part of something larger than myself. But I am reluctant to call it the body of Christ, for that seems to require of each member a confessional yielding, some sort of doctrinal consent such as I made that summer day under the hemlocks in my eleventh year. What I sense rather is Christ working his Father's will that none should perish, Christ gathering all those he would have for himself—and my solidarity with them.

My father. Pete Harris. William J. Barker. The opossum in the woodlot. An anonymous reviewer. Edward Abbey. My grandfather. My grandmother. My offended aunts. Will. The squirrels. The mice. The friends whose lights burn in the valley. The angels of heaven. Al Campbell. My wife. My daughter. The congregation. Creation itself. All pieces of the puzzle. All in the care of the Spirit. Members one of another. The community I cannot escape. The community I mean to speak for.

TWELVE

Three springs break from the hillside.
Like the laughter of children
their waters gather
into the single song of Salvation Brook.
Without ceasing, through the longest days
of summer, its clear voice gives
its Maker praise.

Beside its hemlock shadowed pools,
the heart-shaped prints of deer,
mingled with the spoor
of possum, coon, and mouse,
declare such news as people
perish for want of hearing.

Here I would settle into joy,
be found a part of all
that sings such praise.
But I am lost;
the news I hear from distant lands
is news of Peoples dying.

In Bosnia: Death.
In Israel: Death.
In South Africa: Death.
In Los Angeles: Death.
In Haiti: Death.
In Somalia: Death.
In Liberia: Death.
In Grenada, Panama, and Iraq:
Death.

Father of Mercy,
Who shall be found innocent?

Who shall be found
while Christ incarnate suffers
in the flesh He came to save?

Here where all would be well
I am found a part of all I would not be.
Here in the presence of Your creatures
I lift my hostage voice
and keen.

Part Five

Border Life

The Child Is Father of the Man

Boy in a Blind

A God to Thank

In the Presence of Slugs

The Hawk on the Pergola

Border Life

Every walk is a story, a narrative line leading out from home to a point of crisis, change or insight and then back to the known and a time of reflection. The variables of weather, mood and attention make for mystery. No walk, however familiar the territory covered, repeats any other. John Burroughs knew this, and by rambling became the most popular nature writer of the early twentieth century. John Muir walked more expansively, living on bread and water, discovering his and the nation's wildness in the mountains of California and Alaska. Before Burroughs and Muir, Thoreau knew storied walking. Traveling much in Concord, he gave himself up to surprise every day for twenty years.

I began these thoughts while walking one May morning in Letchworth State Park, a narrow thirty-mile strip of old growth and human-fashioned landscape stretched along both sides of the Genesee River gorge in western New York. I had parked my truck beside a bank of trillium at Wolf Creek, crossed the bridge at the lip of the Bridal Veil Falls, and hiked up the hillside above them to a promontory overlooking the mouth of the creek and widening expanse of the gorge. Wolf Creek was swollen with spring runoff, and I had stopped often and turned to gape through the openness of the budding trees for views of the falls that leaves would soon hide. The water plunged too violently for its name, the white lace of its fall too ragged and coarse for any virginal wistfulness. It carved the stone, and what I witnessed in my backward looks was the dark thrust of spring's unchecked drive.

In sun and wind I felt both exhilarated and exposed, so when I walked to the low wall defining the limit of human safety and watched a swallow plummet, wings folded, down out of my sight, then veer suddenly back into view far out over the river, I staggered a bit. Surprised, I knelt, placed my hands on the wall and leaned out to stare down the gray-faced cliff. Though I could hear the tumbling rush of the creek, I couldn't see it. A turkey vulture circled below me, lower and lower, until he, like the swallow, disappeared.

About ten years ago I canoed the Genesee through the gorge with three friends. For most of that morning a vulture had eyed us from the height of his lazy thermal ride. When we had come out of the white water of the Great Bend where two of my friends had been dumped by the tricky currents, we drifted, drying out and laughing about mortality. As we floated close to the gorge wall, I looked up. A man and a woman stood at the point I now occupied. Suddenly one of them stooped, lifted something and hurled it over the edge. A helpless, silent scream ripped at my throat as I realized a baby stroller was hurtling down, bouncing off the near sheer wall. When a limp form separated from the stroller and fell by itself, my scream tore free. My friends turned and looked. A doll plunged into the water beside us.

Laughter echoed from the point, and the couple ran off. Shaking, we paddled to the stroller and doll, lifted them into the canoe and carried them with us through the gorge.

Haunted by the memory, I stood, stepped back and started up the trail to the Great Bend Overlook a mile uphill. As I walked, I asked myself, "Why do I—with my fear of heights growing as my body succumbs to age and gravity—choose so regularly to walk the edge of this gorge?"

The trail stayed well away from the edge, but there were worn paths to unprotected vantages where one could stare down fear. Compelled by my questioning, I took each of them. Finally, standing with my arm around a tree, I got a sort of answer. In the sanctuary of the park, where trails and walls are clear, I wander at the meeting point of my need for safety and my need for the wild, and I rejoice in both.

In his great essay "Walking," Thoreau examines the human need for the wild. For Thoreau the wild is what the gorge is to me; it is the boundless, the extravagant, and it corresponds to some part of the human spirit that I know instinctively must be kept alive. For Thoreau walking is a sacred pilgrimage. He reflects on the word *saunter* and creates an imaginary etymology for it. He ties it to the French phrase *a la Sainte Terre,* to the Holy Land, used to describe those wanderers during the Middle Ages who begged while supposedly traveling to the Holy Land, and he writes,

"They who never go to the Holy Land in their walks, as they pretend, are indeed mere idlers and vagabonds." He adds, a paragraph later,

> We should go forth on the shortest walk, perchance, in the spirit of undying adventure, never to return—prepared to send back our embalmed hearts only as relics to our desolate kingdoms. If you are ready to leave father and mother, and brother and sister, and wife and child and friends, and never see them again—if you have paid your debts, and made your will, and settled your affairs, and are a free man, then you are ready for a walk.

Though I planned to be home for lunch, Thoreau was on my mind as I walked—and so was the Holy Land. Thoreau's language is clearly biblical. But it is not conventional, and exactly what he means when he writes *Holy Land* is as elusive as his use of the word *wild.*

The Holy Land metaphor, however, is quite specific in my imagination, for I was raised to be a Christian. Consequently I associate it with being chosen by God to receive not only a vision but an overwhelming responsibility—the stewardship of his creation; the Holy Land does not come free; God demands things of those who would be his people.

Moses comes first to my mind. Before he became the commanding prophet of the exodus, he was a bumbling huddle of fear conversing with a voice hidden in a burning bush ordering him to remove his shoes for the ground was holy—holy because God was present.

From a later testament another word comes to me. God, in Christ, is incarnate in the world. Theologians tell me incarnation means God, for all eternity, has bound himself to the creation; he has chosen to be the same stuff we are—the same stuff that the Genesis story makes clear is the stuff of the earth itself.

Though what else incarnation might finally mean remains a mystery, one thing is plain: everything is profoundly connected—divinity, humans, vultures, trees, rocks and water. If it is the presence of the divine that sanctifies the ground and divinity has linked itself to all things, then everywhere one walks is holy ground, and the journey to the Holy Land is a journey into awareness. We owe the creation and the Creator attention.

These thoughts began as I walked, but most of the time I was mindless, absorbed in my senses. Light played about me, striking my eye, turning me around, catching my glancing curiosity—never quite letting me see clearly what a moment before had been plain in the dappled morning.

Birds surrounded me—swallows and pigeons diving into the gorge, turkey vultures silent in the sky and songbirds deep in the trees, teasing me, never visible, their songs retreating and moving as I sought their bodies. I recognized the cries of the chickadees and the territorial bluster of the cardinals. Other songs were familiar but unattached in my mind to any particular singer. One song was a short burst so like a wolf whistle I began to look for dryads in the wavering shadows. On the ground I spotted more trillium. Higher in a leaning beech I located a red-bellied woodpecker working a hollow branch, and in a hemlock rising from below the rim of the gorge, I saw a tiny red and orange bird I'm guessing was an American redstart.

As I searched for birds and dryads, I continued my climb toward the Great Bend Overlook. Though the direction of the trail was up, it rolled and fell unevenly along the gorge rim and made for much easier, more pleasant walking than the steep road I drove to my starting point would have made. As I approached the overview and the halfway point of my hike, however, the trail grew steep. For one hundred yards, I felt my heart pumping, laboring to keep up with my ascent. I slowed, but I did not stop. When I came out onto the near flat at the overlook, my heart steadied, my breathing quieted, and I looked into the eye of a vulture soaring along the rim. It was a cold eye, studying me without sympathy. "Not today, fellow," I said. "My heart is pure, and my feet are staying on the narrow path laid down before my birth." Disgusted, he sheared off and dropped to a bloated deer on the river bank 550 feet below.

I pulled off my day pack and settled on a bench placed between a struggling azalea and the waist-high wall. Sitting there with a cup of coffee and a book I did not open, I could see only the sky, but that was fine. A few puffy clouds and the satiated vulture or one of his friends floated above me. Life seemed very good, and I thought I'd finished my walk, come to the point of the turnabout and had nothing before me but the quick drop back to my truck and the dilatory ride home. I looked forward to indulging the right of my white beard, Florida Marlins ball cap and rusty truck to drive as slowly as I wanted.

But there was more to come.

Though I was alone on the rim, I heard laughter. I went to the wall and looked over. Far below me and maybe three hundred yards upriver a drift of rafters bounced and twisted through the roughest course of the river. Through my binoculars I watched the supple rafts rise and fall, their middles bent high above their ends, their riders, soaked, hanging on and screaming, having the time of their lives. A few kayakers accompanied the rafters. They had the advantage of paddling back upstream and repeating the thrill. One paddler rolled his kayak three times trying to negotiate a chute between two rocks before getting it right and putting on speed to catch the rafters approaching the next cascade.

The vulture, ever watchful, continued to circle, periodically looming overhead, dropping his shadow on me. I remembered reading that their sense of smell is relatively undeveloped and that they find carrion with their eyes. I tired of watching the rafters, so I gathered my thermos and book, stuffed them in my day pack and headed back down the trail, quickly outpacing the rafters.

For me going downhill is the harder part of walking; it strains my beat-up knees. Every time I've fallen and injured myself, I've been going downhill, but it seems that downhill is always the way home, and once I loop away I've got to face the return. The steep slope proved short. Looking back on it I wondered that I had been winded climbing, but I knew the truth of my body and did not wonder long.

A movement caught my eye, and I stopped. The woods were still. Then what looked like a dark leaf rose from the woods floor, fluttered drunkenly first left, then right and landed twenty feet away. I knew it instantly—a mourning cloak butterfly.

I found it through my binoculars and brought it close enough to see the shining blue line and the creamy spots edging its wings. I lowered the binoculars and tried to find it with my eye, but I could not. It lay hidden, invisible, in the detritus. I stepped toward where I'd last seen it, and it rose from the dead oak leaves to catch the sunlight momentarily before settling back a few feet farther away. Again, though I marked its landing, I could not find it unaided, and when I moved once more, it launched itself into the extravagant wind and rode its will out over the river where I could not follow.

I stayed far from the edge, keeping my way on the path, but I held the mourning cloak in my eye as I walked. "We hug the earth,—how rarely we mount!" Thoreau writes near the end of "Walking." In another place he complained, "I feel that with regard to Nature I live a sort of border life on the confines of a world into which I make occasional and transient forays only." Far earlier in his life than the schoolroom reader might think, Thoreau gave up his Emersonian attempt to read the hieroglyphs of nature and find in what he saw transcendental meanings. What he sought was an identification with the other.

As I descended toward my truck, I gave up thinking. I simply walked, allowing myself to be taken in by the world I shared with the mourning cloak, the hungry vulture and the raucous rafters seeking excitement. At the promontory where I knelt out of fear rather than reverence for the Holy Land, I stopped to wait for the rafters. There, loafing, taking my sweet time, I began to shape my unfinished walk into this story. The rafters were so long coming, I gave up waiting and left without seeing them again. But the vulture tracking them was in sight. Even when the sky seems empty, he and his brothers and sisters are there; they see a long way.

Back in my truck I turned my memory once more to that couple on the promontory and the tumbling stroller and doll. What perversity could have brought them to that place in the sun that summer afternoon? What were they thinking as, my scream following them, they ran laughing from the edge? To what land, to what end, might they have been pilgrims?

I will never know the answers to those questions. Nor am I likely to comprehend incarnation—how it fits into the web of other Christian fundamentals: sin, redemption and resurrection. But I have learned that mystery is as often suggestive of truth as doctrine is. When my friends and I had canoed the river (after picking up the stroller and doll), we paddled into the mouth of Wolf Creek, pulled our canoes onto shore and walked upstream toward the falls. We did not get all the way to the Bridal Veil; we were stopped by a fall that can't be seen from the trail. At its base we found deep, round holes large enough to hold a tired, hot paddler. But we could not tell if we could stand safely in one or if the bottoms were so far beyond our reach that we would slip beneath the surface unable to rise to breathe. We could have measured their depths with a fallen branch or a piece of driftwood, but we did not. Instead we walked around them and returned to the canoes.

What I have written is one story out of many I might have constructed from the materials of my walk. I tell it because it is a story that helps me live. I have faith in it, for stands in harmony with the great stories of my culture. More than that, it stands in harmony with the story of Scripture informing that culture. As I backed from my parking spot, I could see my morning cloaked in fear and joy, the vulture circling and the trillium dancing just beyond my windshield.

The Child Is Father of the Man

"The child is father of the Man," William Wordsworth wrote, having demonstrated the statement's truth by composing his great autobiographical poem, "The Prelude." Though few of us have Wordsworth's power of recollection, the essential rightness of his insight came home to me recently when I happened on a reference to "the late Thornton Burgess, noted Sandwich naturalist and author."

I remembered Burgess. My mother had read his animal stories to me before I was old enough for school. Reddy Fox, Jimmy Skunk, Joe Otter, Happy Jack the Squirrel and Peter Rabbit jumped, fully clothed and full of mischief, into my sight. But I faltered on the word *naturalist*. Nothing in my memory suggested to me that Burgess was anything other than a seriously dated author of moralistic children's stories.

On the Internet I found a brief biography of Burgess. He was a native Cape Codder, born in Sandwich in 1874. Between 1910, when his first book, *Old Mother West Wind,* appeared, and 1965, the year of his death, he published an astounding fifteen thousand children's stories.

During World War I, his work on behalf of conservation was so effective that more than one million acres were set aside as bird sanctuaries. At the same time his Happy Jack Squirrel Savings Club urged children to purchase War Savings Stamps.

Following the war, he wrote four popular nature guides for children, hosted a national radio broadcast, helped document the life of the last heath hen and became a regular speaker at the Museum of Natural History. Eventually he was awarded an honorary doctorate from Northeastern University and was recognized by the Boston Museum of Science for "leading children down the path to the wide wonderful world of the outdoors."

All this information sent me to the attic, where I found the tattered orange book my mother had read to me. I opened it and read, "Bobby Coon, he of the ragged tail and black mask, is just like everybody else—he makes mistakes. Everybody does, grown-ups as well as boys and girls." The book was just as I remembered it: dreadfully bad, anthropomorphic to the core and charming. No matter how I tried, I could discover no usable natural history in it, nothing to explain the honors lavished on Burgess.

The main clause of the first sentence, however, fascinated me: "Bobby Coon . . . is just like everybody else." I wondered if the anthropomorphism might have served a purpose the ecologically sophisticated miss. Aldo Leopold's land ethic, the ethic at the heart of most environmental philosophies, is predicated on the metaphor of community—the broader our sense of who is a member of the community, the broader our range of concern and sympathy will be. It struck me that children who identify themselves with the creatures, who see the creatures as being like themselves, are more likely to love them than children who hold them at a distance while mastering information about them.

Discussing the failure of environmental education curriculums in our elementary schools, David Sobel of the Antioch New England Graduate School writes in the journal *Orion*, "What's important is that children have an opportunity to bond with the natural world, to learn to love it and feel comfortable in it, before being asked to heal its wounds."

In his 1960 autobiography, *Now I Remember,* Burgess stated he never set out to teach conservation lessons. His intent was to entertain. His conscious teaching entered into his work after he discovered how children react to stories. He tells of receiving a letter from some young boys explaining why they had given up trapping: "The moment these animals, these muskrats were given personality," Burgess writes, "they became a part of the world of these boys and infinitely more interesting alive than dead." He goes on to anticipate Leopold's extension of community to the land: "Arouse [a boy's] interest in the daily lives of the lesser creatures and [a] sense of justice is aroused. He at once becomes their friend and champion."

Sobel agrees. The challenge for parents and educators, he argues, is to help children "develop emotional empathy for the creatures of the natural world." Hearing stories of Happy Jack Squirrel, Grandfather

Frog and the rest of the Green Meadow inhabitants taught me a rudimentary sympathy for my other-than-human neighbors. In Burgess's anthropomorphic animals I saw enough of myself to identify with the living creatures of my yard.

Deeper knowledge of their actual lives came later, in another stage of my development. During that stage I roamed the woods and explored. But the child who learned empathy is the father of the roaming boy and the man who sits remembering and writing.

Boy in a Blind

"A lot of would-be naturalists are just lazy," Robert Michael Pyle writes in *Orion Afield*. He's right. In my case, dead right. Much of what I don't know I don't know because I've squandered my chances to learn. Pyle fortunately cuts me a break when he adds, "Nameless does not mean faceless." Summer after summer, I recognize plants—their shapes and colors—and turn to my wife for the names. She is the one with the disciplined memory. She also remembers bird songs, phone numbers and how to manipulate our computer programs.

Often I wonder what it is in me that so obstinately thwarts my good intentions to learn the names of the things around me, that leaves me pointing, gushing, "Wow! Look at that!" and stuck for words. Sometimes I think whatever it is was born in my childhood.

I am a child of the margin. Growing up, I lived in three houses. Each was built by my father, and each backed up to a woods or a field. When school was out I was set free to roam—first in the close woods, then, as I grew, for unlimited miles. What I sought were high places, places that allowed me to take in expanses of landscape, places that allowed me to see far in safety.

A half mile from the third and last house of my childhood, a series of grown-over strip mines ripped through the rolling Pennsylvania hills exposing shale cliff faces and scree-covered piles of wastes. The stark devastation of that landscape called me, held me and, I believe, shaped me. Without my knowing, it came to represent the whole earth, and in its grip I learned to find joy in the shadows of brokenness.

One cut plunged deeper into the hillside than the others, forming a horseshoe-shaped declivity sheltering a shallow year-round pond, a home for frogs and snakes. My brother and I haunted it—he for the herps, I for the mysterious tracks along its edge. I wanted to know the creatures that made them.

Today any field guide would satisfy my curiosity, but forty-five years ago popular field guides were not available. And I think I would not have been content to read about the makers of those fine hieroglyphs in the mud; I wanted to learn with my own eyes.

I persuaded my mother—my father had said, "Sure"—to let me spend a night watching, perched on the horseshoe rim above the pond. From sticks, broken branches and stalks of weed I built a crude blind. Equipped with sandwiches, juice and a flashlight, I took up my station near dusk with no idea how long the hours until morning might be.

At first nothing happened. The warm summer breeze moved through my blind without stirring the cattails thirty feet below. Then the breeze died, and the light faded. I know the night would have been filled with the music of insects, but I remember it as silent and close. I grew anxious and shined my light on the pond. I saw my light, a cool spot of white reflecting back at me, and nothing more. I turned it out and waited.

And waited.

And waited.

I've forgotten what time I gave up and wound my way back through the broken landscape to home, but my father was still up. "See anything?" he asked.

"Nope," I answered.

"That's how it goes sometimes," he said, teaching me more than I understood.

I didn't make another vigil. I learned a bit about tracking from a Boy Scout handbook and have made it last a lifetime. But I wish I had gone out again in innocence; another night of watching might have changed my life. I think Adam did not give the creatures names. I think the creatures told him their names because he was still enough and stayed long enough to hear their words.

We humans are curious beings. We have inquiring minds, a passion to know that is our glory. We seek to explore the farthest reaches of time and distance. To do that we have invented technologies as simple as telescopes and as complex as language. I am for telescopes and language. But I am also for silence and waiting.

I want to wrap my imagination around a billion years as surely as I want to know a raccoon in a strip mine pond. I want to butt joyfully against the limits of comprehension. But I want even more to remember that knowledge, the kind worth seeking, comes by revelation, and that revelation doesn't come by asking. Like a boy in a blind, we can only be there, open to receive it should it choose to grace us in the dark of night.

A God to Thank

The summer of 1998, what was to be the summer of butterflies, became, almost without my noticing, the summer of thankfulness. Our garden, planted with buddbleia, nicotinia, coneflowers, bee balm and other attracters, was well established. We had feeders, water, basking rocks, and we had binoculars handy—holding the field guide closed in the wind. The butterflies came as we hoped: painted ladies, red and white admirals, tiger swallowtails, cabbage whites, sulphurs, blues and monarchs.

Though I remembered catching, killing and mounting butterflies in my boyhood, the individuals nectaring on my flowers were safe. My only desire was to know more about them. For me that inevitably leads to books. Through July, my wife and I sat on the deck reading life histories and watching. To broaden my reading, I bought a poem sequence, *The Monarchs,* by Alison Hawthorne Deming, the great-great-granddaughter of Nathaniel. I wasn't sure what I was getting when I bought it. I didn't know if it would be God-haunted or simple description. It was neither. It was a complex sequence using the life history of the monarch to examine human experience.

About halfway through it I read these lines:

> Unable to hear, see, smell, or taste,
> they know when to drop their lower branches,
> broaden their root anchor, when to
> climb and bud. The redwoods, without
> liquid hydrogen or God, have mastered time.

I put the book down and stared off at the distant hills. The casual dismissal of God disturbed me. It felt out of place, unnecessary to the poem. Recalling similar passages in Deming's essays, I wondered what Grandfather Nat would think. Then I asked myself what I thought.

Such dismissals occur quite often in the work of recent American nature writers. Biologists seem to lag behind physicists in the discovery of humility. Their thinking smacks of an arbitrariness akin to Bertrand Russell's. In *Why I Am Not a Christian* Russell complained that if something had to be without a cause it might as well be the universe as God. At eighteen that appealed to me. Like the physicists, however, I've discovered that my imagination is a little too small to contain the creation. The appearance of chance—even the operation of chance in the universe—does not rule out a pattern I have not yet discovered—or, more likely, a pattern I cannot discover because I am a part of it.

About the same time I was reading Russell, I was also reading F. Scott Fitzgerald. No paragon of faith, Fitzgerald articulated a much richer idea. He wrote that though he had never desired a God to pray to, he had often desired a God to thank. I missed much of Fitzgerald's wry humor back in the early 1960s, but his remark has stayed with me, and I've come to cherish it. For now I see that if I admit my life is a gift, I also admit that it is received from a gift-giver to whom I owe a debt of gratitude.

A flutter of orange rose above the hedge, dipped down to the nicotinia, lifted quickly and then settled on the bee balm: a monarch. I picked up the binoculars and brought him close to my eyes. He was good to see.

Several months have passed since I watched that butterfly nectar in the sun. As Thanksgiving approaches I find myself wondering how to pay that debt of gratitude I felt and feel for my life. I think I must begin where I am—sitting in my garden study—setting down these words. I know their limitations. They are an inadequate net, ill suited for capturing the wonder I have seen. But they are all I have; I must write or be silent in the presence of glory. Scripture tells me if I choose silence the stones themselves will cry out. Part of me would like to hear their praise. Someday, perhaps, in the fullness of time I will. Meanwhile I offer in thanksgiving and praise these nouns: painted lady, red admiral, tiger swallowtail, mourning cloak, cabbage white, monarch.

In the Presence of Slugs

$\mathcal{M}$y wife and I often watch the PBS comedy *As Time Goes By*. In a recent episode one of the characters, a writer in his sixties, went to the library and took out a stack of books he had always meant to read as a youth. Among those books was *Winnie-the-Pooh*. In a fit of identification I dug my daughter's copy of the "bear of very little brain" from its box in the attic and proceeded to read "Piglet Meets a Heffalump" to my wife. She fell asleep. I can't blame her; it was nearly midnight. Nevertheless, I read to the end.

The story was as charming as I remembered. And a bit more truthful. The heffalump, of course, is an imaginary beast. Piglet's terror, however, and his courage, as he sets out with Pooh to catch one, are real.

Human history is filled with imaginary animals. Saint Augustine declared that the actual existence of an animal is unimportant. What counts is its meaning. Though no scientist is likely to agree, I think he had a point. The heffalump meant danger and adventure to Pooh and Piglet. Real animals, particularly the endangered ones we cherish—lions, elephants, grizzly bears and great whales—play no part in our lives. They are far away from us. They are part of our imagination. We need them for what they stir in us whether we ever see one or not.

A couple of years ago my daughter gave me an exquisitely carved and painted banana slug for Christmas. The gift wasn't a joke. She knew it would renew in me, every time I looked at it, my attraction to the rain forests of the Pacific Northwest. The banana slug is an unlikely candidate for such a role. One would expect an eagle or a whale. Even a seal makes more sense. But I'm a little strange, I guess. I specifically asked for a slug.

Though *Ariolimax columbianus* can grow to twelve inches in length, it is a gentle creature. Slate-green or yellowish, it is spotted with black. Unlike the snail, it is not edible. From the perspectives of both the snail and the diner, this is fortunate. *Helix pomatia*, the original escargot, is now rare and has been largely replaced, at least in the States, by the common garden snail. Imagine great slabs of slug sizzled in butter and garlic.

No. The slug is at its delightful best in the woods blithely motoring at three inches a minute along the trail of slime it dribbles from its chin. Few people find this attribute attractive. But I side with the naturalist Robert Michael Pyle, who writes, "What's so disgusting about mucus? Is it healthy to be so repelled by a vital substance of which we produce rather a lot ourselves?"

The banana slug is territorial. Once you find one, you can find it again and again. Since it prefers the moist wastes of a nurse log in the northwest forests, its territory is almost never a garden. It is hermaphroditic, but it prefers a mate to keep the gene pool swirling and engages in elaborate mating rituals that I won't detail here. Its main work, through a pleasant five-year life, is recycling vegetable matter back into soil. It accomplishes this without being able to chew. All of its teeth—thousands of them—are on its tongue, which it uses as a rasp.

Everything about this slug fascinates me. But I've never seen one. I've looked. I've wandered off the trails and poked around logs and come up empty. For all the evidence my eye has gathered, the banana slug is as imaginary as the heffalump. I'm not much bothered by that. I haven't seen the Loch Ness Monster, Bigfoot or Yeti either. My imagination needs things out there beyond its experience. It needs things to draw it beyond itself into the richness of the world.

One of my favorite contemporary poems is called "To the Unseeable Animal." The Kentucky poet Wendell Berry wrote it in response to a remark his young daughter made. She said, "I hope there's an animal somewhere that nobody has ever seen. And I hope nobody ever sees it."

I agree.

The Hawk on the Pergola

Three hummingbirds, darting and hovering, celebrate a festival of nectar between the feeder and the bee balm. None of them care that Linda and I present obstacles to their drunken flights as we kneel weeding about the sage. They buzz by us like oversized bees, sip, rise straight up, level off at full speed and pull up to rest in the dead spruce shading the garden. There, splendidly indifferent, they preen, drilling their slender beaks into the feathers under their wings, flashing their ruby throats in the sun.

A week ago I put out the sunflower feeders. Though the sparrows and doves remain content to drink and bathe at the shallow end of the pond, goldfinches, chickadees and a single nuthatch began to feed within a day. Starlings have begun to flock, setting up their pecking order and squabbling on the power lines. Soon they will be hanging around pushing and shoving the smaller birds aside, but they won't stay. They never do.

Yesterday afternoon when I looked out the back door, several goldfinches had the small feeder over the pond spinning and swinging. I could see the goldfish among the water lilies, and I assumed the leopard frogs were lurking in their usual spots in the algae around the roots of the sedge. A line of blooming roses led from me to the pond. The butterfly bush rose and fell in the light breeze, and the bee balm stood tall and steady near the hedge.

Surveying the garden, I felt smugly satisfied. What I had called into place by imagination and work was good. Then I looked up.

Atop the pergola built onto the garden shed beyond the pond sat a large hawk. Beneath him the fronds of asparagus, pale green and six feet tall, bowed in unconscious admiration.

I called Linda. Eager for a better look, she eased the door open and stepped slowly onto the deck. Just as slowly, the hawk spread his wings, lifted from his perch, turned and flew lazily toward the trees on the bank beyond the garden. Through binoculars I followed his flight. When he entered the trees and disappeared, I crossed the lawn in pursuit. Though I could hear him, I could not see him. The growth of the trees was too thick. Disappointed, I went back and stood under the pergola. Something of the hawk remained, and I felt the strangeness of his presence in my ordered world.

The asparagus nodded to me, brushing my face, and I turned to it. In the net of its fronds was a wispy catch of gray feathers. I reached out and took one in my hand. Some small bird was gone.

I did not feel the annoyance I feel when the neighbor's cat hunts at my feeder. I felt, rather, a completeness. I found myself wishing I'd come out of the house a few minutes earlier to witness the act, and then I was glad I hadn't. I dropped the feather; sacrament must be a mystery.

For a long while I stood there. I liked the garden I had made. I liked knowing where the hawk that did not wish to be seen waited out my watching.

Today as I kneel in the sage I think of that knowledge as a kind of hope—a hope much like the indifference of the hummingbirds. I can't quite say what it is, but I am convinced it points to a wholeness, a pattern of interaction and meaning I can intuit but never see.

In "Design," his sonnet describing the violent conjunction of a predatory white spider, an innocent flower and a moth, Robert Frost questioned what kind of power would govern a world where such things happen. He asked, "What but design of darkness to appall / If design govern in a thing so small?" He intended us to be appalled.

John Muir opened his narrative of a destructive windstorm in the Sierras in a different frame of mind. He wrote, "The mountain winds, like the dew and rain, sunshine and snow, are measured and bestowed with love on the forests to develop their strength and beauty." I think Muir got it right. Love brought the small bird, the hawk and myself to the yard. It is not for me to find an explanation for it all. Rather it is for me to be found by that love. It does not matter if I am the small bird, the hawk or the mediating observer.

Vow

The need to work this land to fit my wants
I yield. I vow no more to walk with plans
like gossip falling from my mouth. I choose
to go in silence, learning, in my sure
refusal, the truth that yields to yielding.

At Equinox, before the flood of light
sets water loose, I covenant to give
the downward rush beneath the grass its head.
I'll dam no stream. I'll dig no pond. Nor will
I plant willows to suck the wet spots dry.

My work shall be to say the nature
of Creation's slow unfolding, to name what
becoming new has always been, to praise
what lives without my praise unto itself.

Bibliography

Berry, Wendell. *The Long-Legged House.* New York: Harcourt, Brace & World, 1969.

———. *Standing by Words.* San Francisco: North Point, 1983.

Frost, Robert. *Selected Prose of Robert Frost.* Edited by Hyde Cox and Edward Connery. New York: Collier, 1968.

Eliot, T. S. "Tradition and the Individual Talent." In *The Sacred Wood: Essays on Poetry and Criticism.* London: Methuen, 1960.

Gardner, John. *On Becoming a Novelist.* New York: Harper & Row, 1983.

Merton, Thomas. *Conjectures of a Guilty Bystander.* Garden City, N.Y.: Doubleday, 1966.

———. *No Man Is an Island.* New York: Harcourt, Brace, 1955.

———. "Poetry and the Contemplative Life." In *Figures for an Apocalypse.* Norfolk, Conn.: New Directions, 1948.

———. *Secular Journal.* New York: Farrar, Straus & Cudahy, 1959.

———. *The Seven Storey Mountain.* New York: Harcourt, Brace, 1948.

———. *The Sign of Jonas.* New York: Harcourt, Brace, 1953.

———. *Thirty Poems.* Norfolk, Conn.: New Directions, 1944.

O'Connor, Flannery. *Mystery and Manners: Occasional Prose.* New York: Farrar, Straus & Giroux, 1969.

Rice, Edward. *The Man in the Sycamore Tree: The Good Times and Hard Life of Thomas Merton, an Entertainment with Photographs.* Garden City: N. Y.: Doubleday, 1970.

Seerveld, Calvin. *A Christian Critique of Art and Literature.* Toronto: Association for Reformed Scientific Studies, 1968.

Stafford, William. "A Way of Writing." In *A Writer's Reader.* 6th ed. Edited by Donald Hall and D. L. Emblen. New York: HarperCollins, 1991.

Thoreau, Henry David. *Walden.* With an introduction and annotations by Bill McKibben. Boston: Beacon, 1997.

————. "Walking." In *Wild Apples and Other Natural History Essays.* Edited by William Rossi. Athens: University of Georgia Press, 2002.

Works by John Leax

POETRY BOOKS

Reaching into Silence: Poems. Wheaton, Ill.: Harold Shaw, 1974.

The Task of Adam. Grand Rapids, Mich.: Zondervan, 1985.

Country Labors: Poems for All Seasons. Grand Rapids, Mich.: Zondervan, 1991.

POETRY CHAPBOOKS

A Proper Reticence. kattadn molehill pamphlets, 1971.

Finding the Word. Being Publications, 1972.

The Screen of Nature. Lanthorn Publications, 1972.

Meditations on the Alphabet. Grafiktrakt, 1977).

Shoring the Ruins. For the Time Being 6:4, 1978.

The Falls Discipline. Lanthorn Publications, n.d.

FICTION

Nightwatch. Grand Rapids, Mich.: Zondervan, 1989.

PROSE

In Season and Out. Grand Rapids, Mich.: Zondervan, 1985.

Standing Ground: A Personal Story of Faith and Environmentalism. Grand Rapids, Mich.: Zondervan, 1991.

Grace Is Where I Live: Writing as a Christian Vocation. 1st ed. Grand Rapids, Mich.: Baker, 1993.

Out Walking: Reflections on Our Place in the Natural World. Grand Rapids, Mich.: Baker, 2000.

Also Available

Grace Is Where I Live Audio Book
Selected readings by John Leax on one audio CD. Includes:

What I Have Found
Holiness and Craft
Sabbatical Journal, Sections 3 and 10
In the Care of the Spirit, Sections 1, 3, 6, 7 and 11
Border Life
Boy in a Blind
The Hawk on the Pergola

Grace Is Where I Live Enhanced Ebook
Includes both the Audio Book and a second CD containing the complete text of the revised and expanded edition (PDF), additional selected readings, photos, links, background information and more!

Available online at www.wordfarm.net

About John Leax

John Leax is professor of English and poet-in-residence at Houghton College in Houghton, New York. His articles, fiction and poems have been widely published in anthologies and in periodicals such as *Image, The Christian Century, The Other Side, The Cresset, The Reformed Journal, Christianity Today, ISLE, Christianity and Literature, Radix, Cold Mountain Review* and *Midwest Quarterly.*

His books of poetry include *Reaching into Silence* (1974), *The Task of Adam* (1985) and *Country Labors* (1991). His novel, *Nightwatch,* was published in 1989. And his non-fiction works include *In Season and Out* (1985), *Standing Ground* (1991) and *Out Walking* (2000). *Grace Is Where I Live,* published originally in 1993, was reissued in a revised and expanded edition by WordFarm in 2004.

Leax gives several readings and lectures each year at various colleges, libraries and conferences. He has read at Calvin College, Concordia College, Nyack College, The Kings College, Asbury Theological Seminary, Gordon College, St. Joseph's College, SUNY Buffalo and others. He has been featured as a panelist and seminar leader at Calvin College's biannual Festival of Faith & Writing.

He is a member of the Conference on Christianity and Literature, The Chrysostom Society, The Orion Society, The Association for the Study of Literature and the Environment and the Nature Conservancy.

Leax is also an avid gardener.